THE STORY OF WORLD MYTHOLOGIES

THE STORY OF WORLD MYTHOLOGIES

From Indigenous Tales to Classical Legends

Terri-ann White

ARCTURUS

A note from the author:
I would like to give my thanks to Georgina Gregory for her research assistance.

A note on this text:
'Mesoamerica' is a term used by archaeologists and anthropologists to refer to Mexico and neighbouring countries in Central America in the period prior to European contact. The peoples who inhabited this region before the arrival of Europeans were incredibly diverse. Nevertheless, archaeologists see a number of cultural connections that distinguish ancient Mesoamericans from ancient North Americans and South Americans. Thus, the ancient civilizations of Mexico, Guatemala, Belize, El Salvador, Honduras, Nicaragua and Costa Rica may all be deemed Mesoamerican.
　　[from *World History Encyclopedia* by Alfred J. Andrea © 2011 Copyright ABC-CLIO LLC]

ARCTURUS

This edition published in 2017 by Arcturus Publishing Limited
26/27 Bickels Yard, 151–153 Bermondsey Street,
London SE1 3HA

Copyright © Arcturus Holdings Limited

All rights reserved. No part of this publication may be reproduced, stored in a retrieval system, or transmitted, in any form or by any means, electronic, mechanical, photocopying, recording or otherwise, without prior written permission in accordance with the provisions of the Copyright Act 1956 (as amended). Any person or persons who do any unauthorised act in relation to this publication may be liable to criminal prosecution and civil claims for damages.

Senior Editor: Daniel Conway
Art Director: Peter Ridley
Designers: Dani Leigh and James Pople

ISBN: 978-1-78428-643-9
AD005416UK

Printed in China

Contents

Introduction	10
Myths, legends, and folklore	12
What is the difference between myths, legends and folk stories?	14
Writing, reading and collecting myths	15
Common features	16
What do myths tell us?	17
Creation myths	18
The Dreamtime *(Australia)*	20
The seven generations of the age of gods *(Japan)*	22
The Island of Creation *(Egypt)*	24
Marduk: the killing of the goddess *(Mesopotamia)*	26
The cosmic egg *(Finland)*	28
The song of the birth of the world *(Estonia)*	30
The lands pulled up from the sea by a giant fish hook *(Polynesia)*	32
The Vedic creation myth *(India)*	34
The creative sacrifice *(China and Indonesia)*	36
The Aztec creation myth *(Mexico)*	38
The universality of 'the serpent' *(World mythologies)*	40
Men as birds and women as fish *(Korea)*	42
The origin of fire and light *(World mythologies)*	44
Great floods	46
Noah and the Ark *(Middle East)*	48
The tree god myth *(Korea)*	50
Nanabozho and the Great Serpent *(North America)*	52
The Creator's pipe *(North America)*	53
The Great Flood and Yu the Great *(China)*	54
Cosmology	56
The world as evil *(Persia)*	58
The battle of good and evil *(Middle East)*	60

Yoruba philosophy   *(Nigeria)* 62

Yggdrasil: the world tree   *(Scandinavia)* 64

The sky ladder   *(World mythologies)* 66

Sun and moon   *(World mythologies)* 68

Tribal gods   *(Scandinavia)* 70

Stealing the sun   *(Congo)* 72

The origins of the seasons   *(North America)* 74

Time   *(World mythologies)* 76

STORIES OF GODS AND MEN 78

Poseidon   *(Greece)* 80

Achilles   *(Greece)* 82

Zeus and his thunderbolts   *(Greece)* 84

The Trojan War   *(Greece)* 86

Marrying mortals   *(Greece)* 88

Pele's revenge   *(Hawaii)* 90

The maid of the mist   *(North America)* 92

War with the Titans   *(Greece)* 94

Devas against Asuras   *(India)* 96

Celtic gods against the Fomorians   *(Ireland)* 98

Conflict and competition   *(Greece)* 100

Osiris, Isis and Horus against Set   *(Egypt)* 102

Mount Olympus   *(Greece)* 104

Asgard   *(Scandinavia)* 106

Tripartite God of Christianity   *(Middle East)* 108

Vishnu and his avatars   *(India)* 110

The dying god   *(Greece)* 112

Judaeo-Christian God   *(Middle East)* 114

The sky father   *(World mythologies)* 116

Shamanism *(World mythologies)*

    Soyot shamanism *(Siberia)* 118

    Amazonian/Peruvian shamanism *(Amazon basin/Peru)* 119

    Celtic shamanism *(Britain)* 120

    Medicine people *(North America)* 122

    Shamans of the Dogon *(Mali)* 124

Legendary heroes and fantastical creatures and events 126

Defeating the beast *(Greece)* 128
Monkey *(China)* 132
The adventures of Okuninushi *(Japan)* 134
Koschei the Deathless *(Russia)* 136
Vampires, demons and spirits *(World mythologies)* 138
Prince Igor and Krak *(Russia and Poland)* 140
Dragons *(World mythologies)* 142
The Apocalypse *(World mythologies)* 144
    Four Horsemen of the Apocalypse *(Middle East)* 145
    Ragnarok *(Scandinavia)* 146
    Shiva destroys the world *(India)* 148
    Return of the Spider Woman *(North America)* 150

Tricksters 152

Coyote and Raven *(North America)* 154
Anansi *(Ghana)* 156
Reynard the fox *(Europe)* 158
Crow *(Australia)* 160
Robin Hood *(Britain)* 162
Leprechauns *(Ireland)* 164
Kitsune *(Japan)* 166
Ivan the Fool *(Russia)* 168

Mythological epics 170

Beowulf *(Scandinavia)* 172
The Iliad and the Odyssey *(Greece)* 174
Gilgamesh *(Mesopotamia)* 176
Tuatha dé Danann *(Ireland)* 178
Mabinogion *(Britain)* 180
The Popul Vuh *(Mesoamerica)* 182

Death and the afterlife 184

Heaven and hell *(World mythologies)* 186
Valhalla *(Scandinavia)* 188
Orpheus and Eurydice *(Greece)* 190

    Izanagi in the underworld   *(Japan)* 192
    The Heavenly Civil Service   *(China)* 194
    Tuonela, Land of the Dead   *(Finland)* 196
    The lingering spirits and ghosts   *(Africa)* 198
    The River Styx and the underworld   *(Greece)* 200
    Rebirth cycles and the next Life   *(World mythologies)* 202

BLURRING HISTORY, LEGEND AND MYTHOLOGY 204

    Manco Cápac: the legendary founder of the Inca dynasty   *(Peru)* 206
    King Arthur   *(Britain)* 208
    The Ulster Cycle and Fenian Cycle   *(Ireland)* 210
    Bran the Blessed   *(Britain)* 212
    Romulus and Remus   *(Italy)* 214
    The founding of Athens   *(Greece)* 216
    Wolf, mother of the Turks   *(Turkey)* 218
    Viracocha and the founding of Cuzco   *(Peru)* 220
    The Jade Emperor   *(China)* 222

CUSTOMS AND POPULAR RELIGION 224

    Vision quests   *(North America)* 226
    Feng Shui   *(China)* 228
    Animism   *(World mythologies)* 230
    Divination and fortune-telling   *(World mythologies)* 232
    Huacas: monuments of holiness   *(South America)* 234
    Quetzalcoatl as an incarnation of Jesus   *(Mesoamerica)* 236
    Witchcraft and sorcery   *(World mythologies)* 238
    Vodou   *(West Africa)* 240
    Ancestor worship   *(World mythologies)* 242

CONCLUSION 244

BIBLIOGRAPHY 246

PICTURE CREDITS 248

INDEX 252

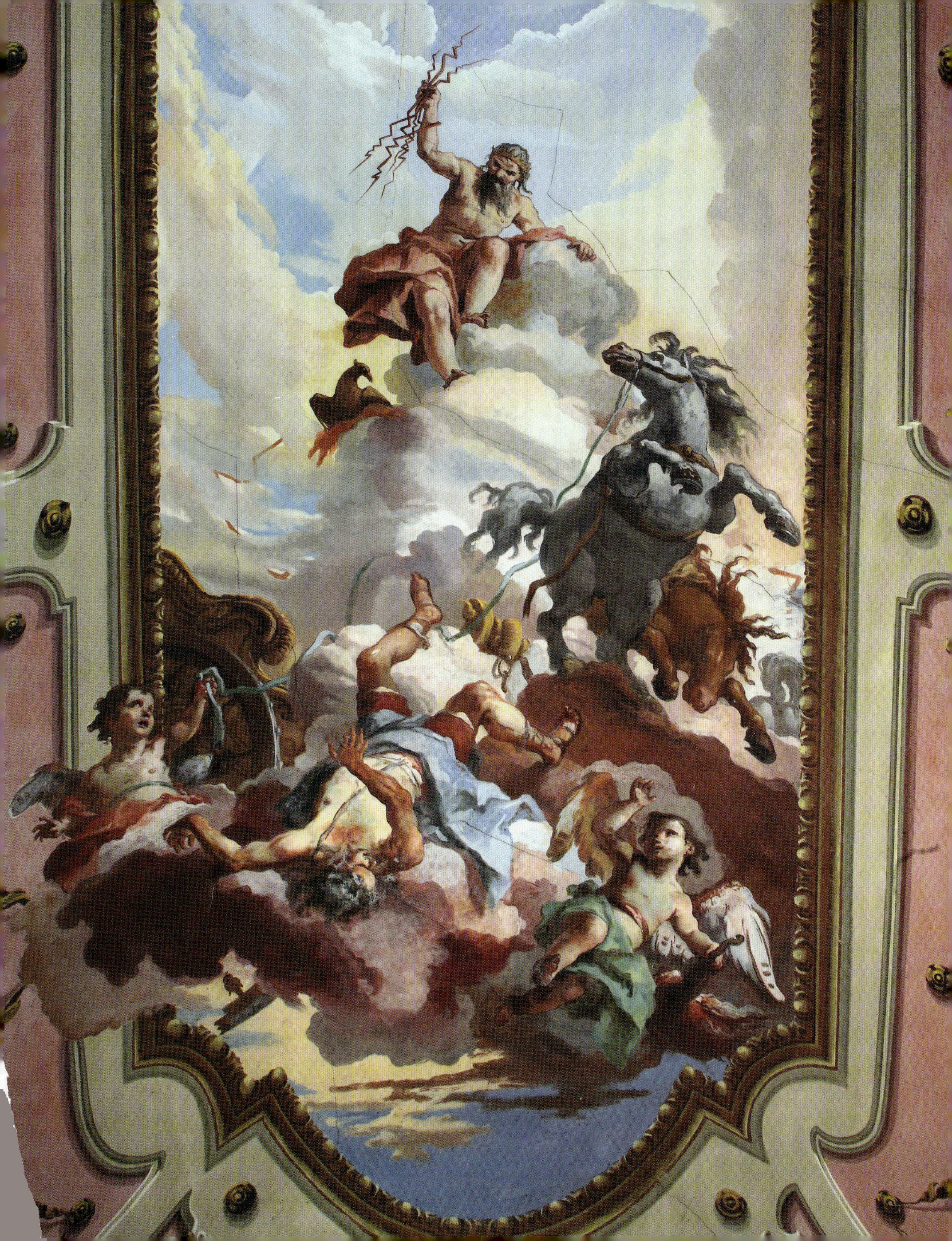

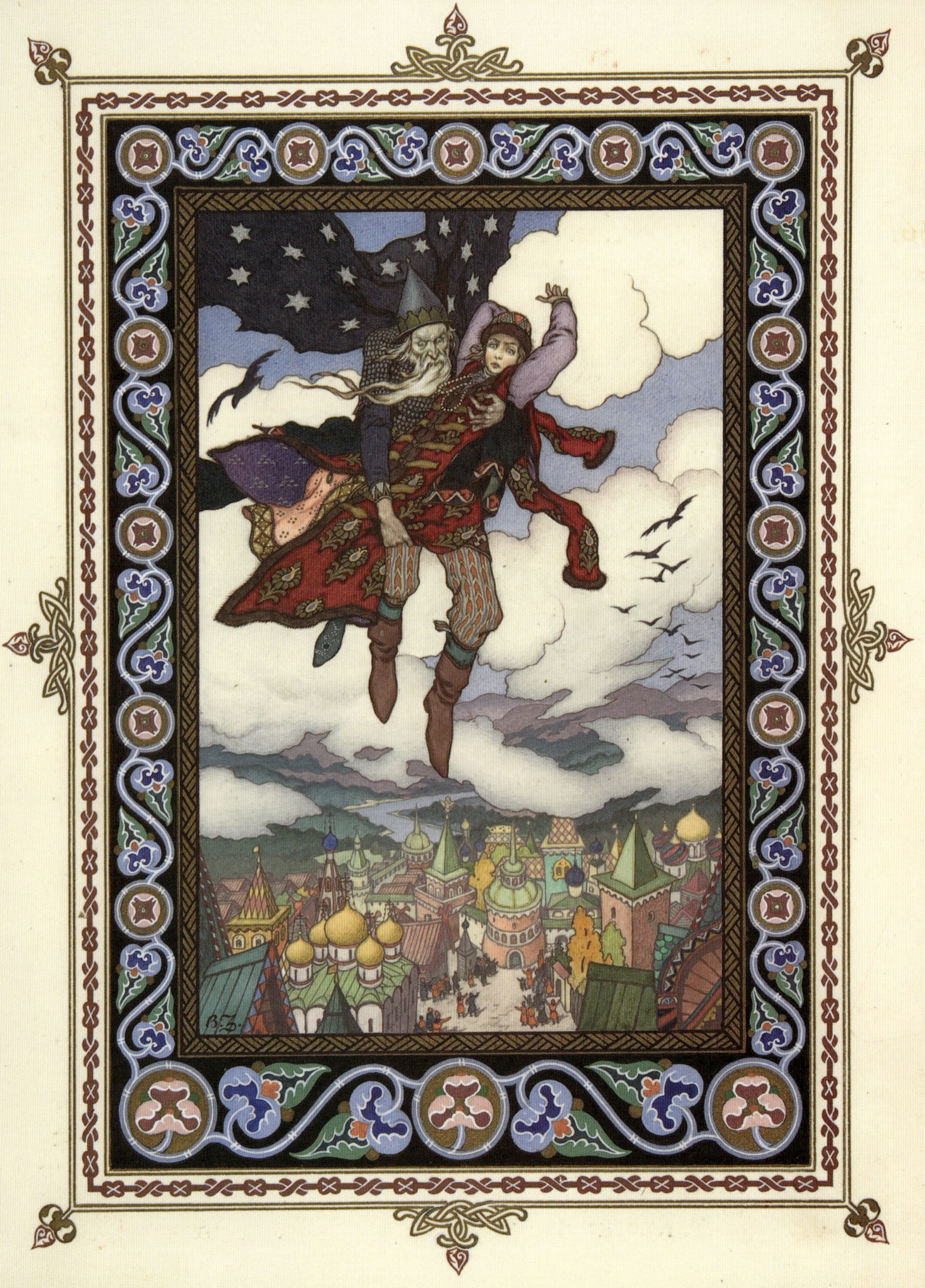

Introduction

There is a magnificent drive in the story-telling and drama of world mythology. It is so easy to lose yourself in these exotic and extravagant worlds. They look so very different from the world of our own times, and yet we can still find many features in common – if we look hard enough. In relation to landscapes, geology, extreme weather events and the murderous inclinations that can rise to the surface in even the most loving families, nothing much has changed with the passage of time, despite the sophistication of modern society resulting from the knowledge and experience we have acquired over many thousands of years.

Some of the oldest myths still told and believed today were created by the first inhabitants of Australia. Some 60,000 years before the invention of the GPS navigation device, Aboriginal tribes mapped their vast continent and ascribed to it a deeply symbolic order that set down both pragmatic advice – for example, how to find food and water in order to stay alive in such a harsh and arid land – and a system of moral and ethical codes that covered all forms of behaviour from sexual reproduction to sharing social responsibility. These beliefs and moral codes are still evident in paintings and carvings made on cave walls, rocks and other surfaces dating from many thousands of years ago.

When reading about the mythologies of other peoples and ancient cultures we need to suspend disbelief and mentally inhabit these other worlds, something humans continue to be good at. In these myths, the worlds of gods, humans and animals are inextricably entwined. Even seas and mountains are capable of independent thought and action, and other life forces – not necessarily recognized today – also have a part to play. While the rational modern mind may have difficulty believing this phantasmagorical world, there are truths contained within the stories, if you look for them. From early childhood to the sunset of life, humans have taken great pleasure and reassurance from made-up tales. This may in part be a retreat from reality, especially when the real world seems so dangerous, and that is no doubt why myths were created in the first place. They gave comfort and confidence to our ancestors in understanding the fearsome forces of earth, sea and sky that affected their lives.

Many world mythologies are now read purely as fiction and enjoyed solely for the beauty of their poetic nature, yet there are numerous insights into psychology and human survival that can be gained from these writings. For example, conflict and competition between the gods is central to many mythologies and designed to teach mortals important lessons about life.

Mythology gives us a direct connection with our human lineage, taking us out of the bubble of our modern clock-driven lives and into a narrative where time is elastic. Through these stories, we can see how immensely our ideas of the world have changed – and how we have too.

第九一年都帝王
第二七日初江王
第八百日平正王
第三七日宋帝王
第六七日變成王
第五七日閻羅王
南无道明和尚
南无金毛師子

Myths, legends and folk stories

Myths, legends and folk stories all have certain characteristics in common, but each one is a separate historical storytelling form that serves a specific purpose. These tales help to satisfy our need to know more about our past and our ancestors.

What is the difference between myths, legends and folk stories?

A myth is a traditional story that endures over generations, or over centuries. It could be about an event; about a person or people; or a subtle guide on how to conduct oneself in life and the consequences of not following society's rules. Myths are about good deeds and bad and about decisions that have disastrous consequences. There are some clear-cut ways to introduce the idea of what a myth is, but there are some grey areas too.

Myths provide a symbolic account of how the world was made and how humans and other sentient beings first formed. They can also tell us how nations and empires developed. Myths commonly describe personality traits and emotional states, indeed the whole gamut of human psychology, often showing aberrant human behaviour in an exaggerated form in order to emphasize a point.

Legends sit within the folklore of a culture. They take the form of historical fact that may also carry some sense of magical power or miraculous potential. Think of legends such as that of Perseus, who destroyed the monster Medusa, or Robin Hood, who had a mission to redistribute wealth and improve the lives of the poor. Each is rooted in the real with actions resulting from defiance of authority or the powerful, or empathy for the underdog, but each is also enhanced by an extra power of the supernatural.

Folk stories carry significant values, traditions and styles that any culture or group of people (a tribe, community or nation) follows over time. They are rich stories with deep insights into human behaviour and expression in words, art and music.

Writing, reading and collecting myths

As may be expected for a storytelling tradition that evolved to make sense of the world for ancient peoples, there are many disagreements to be had about authenticity and authorship. Many myths have been handed down orally over centuries and ingrained into the psyche of the people, but some are younger than that and were imposed upon the culture through recording and analysis by observers such as anthropologists and ethnographers. It can be impossible to unwind some of the detail of such myths in order to distinguish the imported from the authentic that has been recorded, after all, from the people themselves.

There is a seemingly unquenchable thirst to read about mythology that remains powerful even in the digital age of today. Libraries hold numerous books of specific mythologies, while web pages can offer the most baffling interpretations and rereadings, sometimes tailored to affirm mystical or spiritual beliefs or, occasionally, nationalistic or political agendas.

Common features

Each myth, legend and folk story handed down to us or created in our own time contains an original author or group authorship. They are also all interpreted and reworked by each successive generation. The way those stories are recorded shows the reworking starkly. We find a network of variations on a theme, all of them with similar features but there is often an argument about the details. That is the nature of humanity: arguing in the town square, debating in the *agora* (Greek open market), or discussing ideas around a communal fire. In the 21st century, this reworking continues, particularly in literary works, films and digital games. Many people know more about other cultures and their history from such popular forms of media than ever before.

What do myths tell us?

Myths tell us much about the past, present, and sometimes the future. They form a digest of sorts about humanity and the part it plays in the natural world.

Because myths are often presented in a fairly simple manner, they are accessible to a wide-ranging readership and so can be enjoyed for their entertainment value alone. But they are also vehicles of profound knowledge and so warrant a second reading for the messages embedded within them. One such area is in the protocols and taboos relating to all aspects of social life and especially for life, love and war.

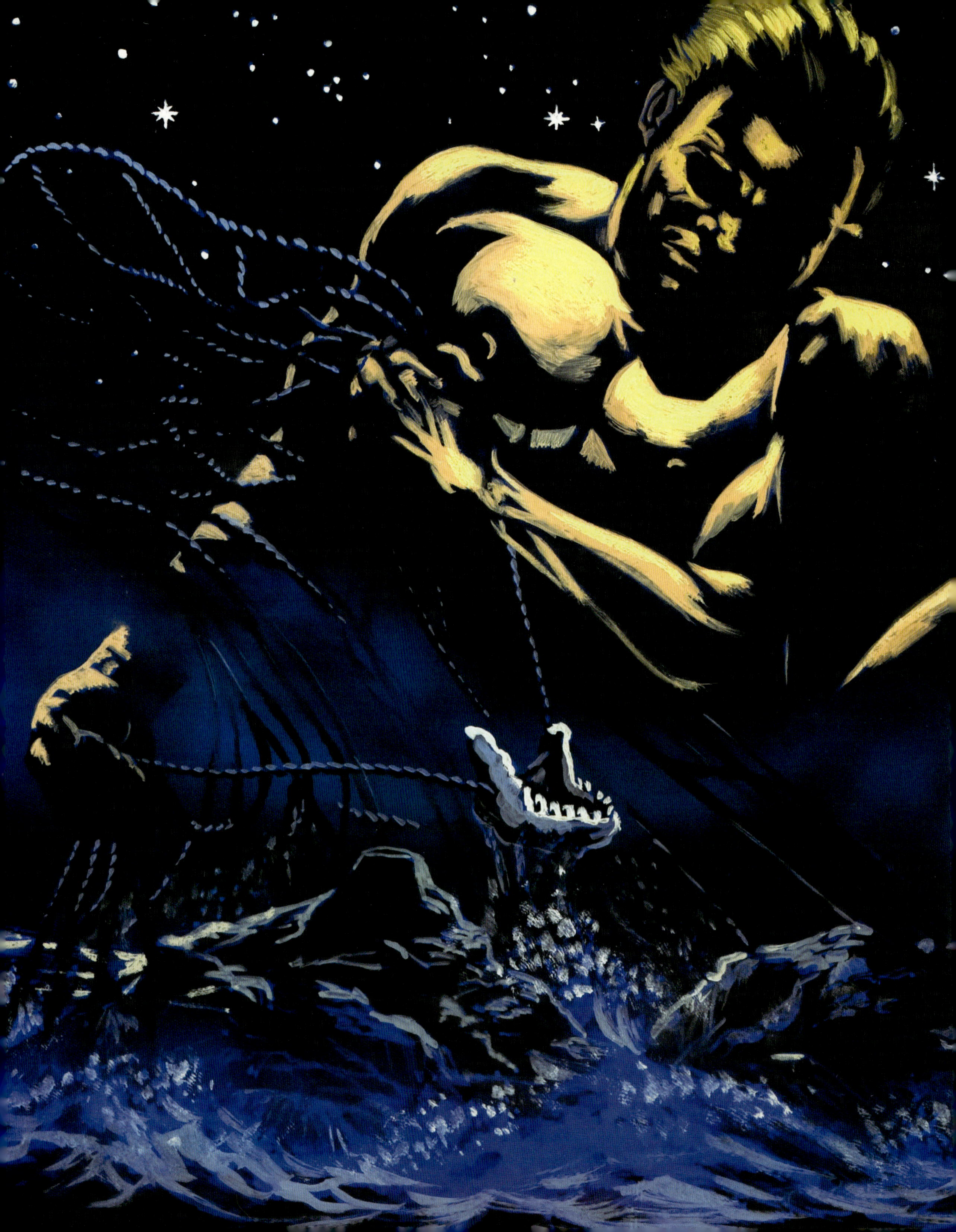

Creation myths

Sit on the top of a mountain or on a ship in the middle of an ocean and you realize just how hard it is to relate to the scale of the world and to understand how it was all formed. Massive land formations, vast bodies of water, and the immense expanse of the sky all seem so huge and timeless and our own lives so puny and brief in comparison. No surprise then that humans have needed some way to understand the part they play in it all.

Our ancestors used our natural human gift for storytelling to make sense of their place in this dramatic world where life could be taken away in the crash of a giant wave, the flash of a storm, or the whims of a cruel king. As with most myths, those describing creation also set down rules of behaviour, outlining taboos and providing guidelines for society to follow.

THE DREAMTIME
AUSTRALIA

Aboriginal people have occupied the island continent of Australia for close to 60,000 years. It therefore provides a rich case study of how creation myths and other myths form and are sustained over an extended time period with minimal influence from outsiders. Australian Aboriginal belief centres around a concept known as 'Dreamtime' or 'Dreaming', which describes a 'golden age' when the land was inhabited by their ancestors – often heroic or supernatural figures. It was these ancestors who devised the rules that Aboriginal people still follow today. The Aboriginal people were (and still are) a hunter-gatherer people, scattered across the country, who mostly live in extended family groups with their own languages.

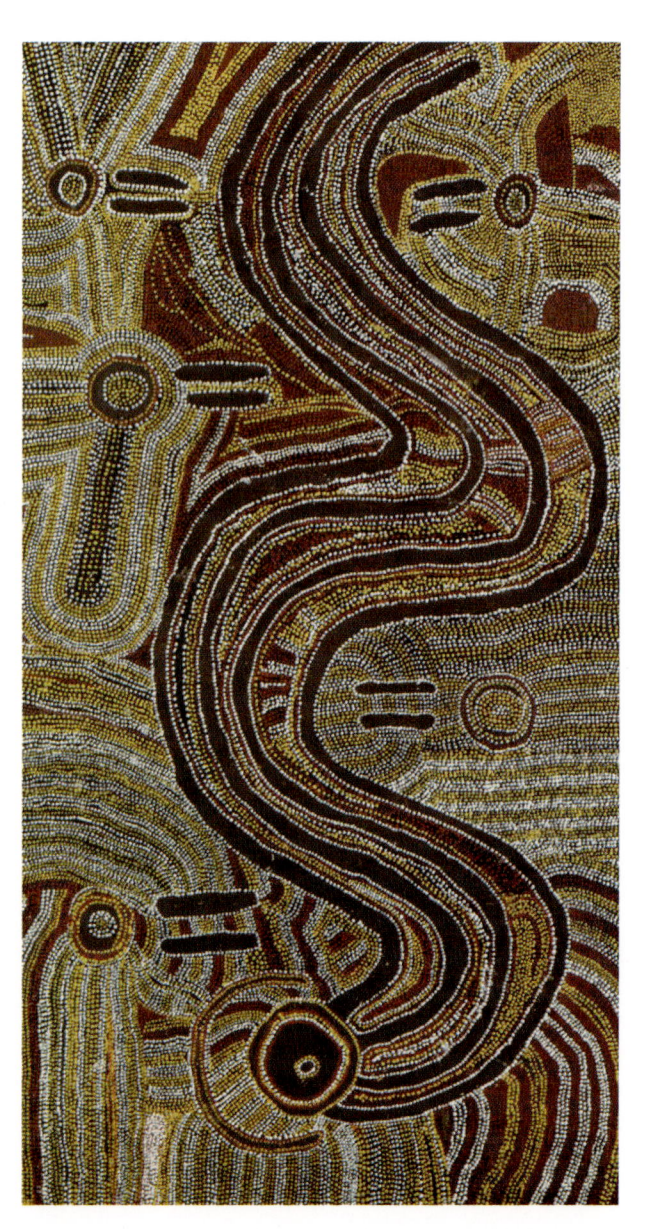

The Dreamtime is a crucial element of daily life and the symbolic counterweight to basic survival. The symbolic work of the Dreamtime is animated in ceremonies that include song and dance, and the elevation of sacred objects used in the dance – literally as well as figuratively – above the heads of the participants. The origin myths are variations on a set of themes and vary according to region but have remained remarkably consistent across groups who have had no contact with one another.

The beginning of the creation myth introduces enormous spirit-beings that traversed and literally made the country with geographical shapes and plants and the spirits of all future people. When sacred spaces were entered they contained a profound community of past and future members of the group the Aboriginal people belonged to.

The Dreamtime was (and is) a deeply sophisticated system of reading the country. Each group holds responsibility for knowing its own country intimately and maintaining this symbolic force. They make maps of the sacred waterholes, hills and other places. The brilliance of this system is that each group has its own unique knowledge informed by an oral mythic tradition. The sum effect is a complete map of the continent, stitched together by the knowledge of individual groups, like a quilt is made up of different panels.

Ngapa Jukurrpa (Water Dreaming), 1987, *by Topsy Nampijinpa Robertson of the Warlpiri people in the Northern Territory, Australia.*

CREATION MYTHS

Aboriginal rock art depicts figures of Mimi Spirits on a cave wall in Kakadu National Park, Northern Territory, Australia.

These creation myths are entirely focused on the land. There are Water Dreaming stories, and myths generated by yams and other plant foods. By attending to the physical places to ensure they remain fresh and accessible and conducting ceremonies around them, the Aboriginal culture keeps the memory of these stories alive.

One Water Dreaming story, *Ngapa Jukurrpa*, belongs to the Warlpiri people of the Tanami Desert. It tells how two rainmaker men sang the rain, unleashing a giant storm that collided with another storm. The two storms travelled across the country. A brown falcon (Kirrkarlanji) carried the storm further west, until the bird dropped it and formed an enormous lake (maliri). Whenever it rains, hundreds of bush ducks (Ngapangarlpa) still flock to that lake, and a soakage still exists there today.

The Dreamtime

The seven generations of the age of gods

Japan

The Kamiyonanayo are the seven generations of god, deity, or divine spirit (*kami*) that emerged after the formation of heaven and earth.

In Shinto, Kotoamatsukami is the collective name for the first gods who were born in Takamagahara (the world of heaven) at the time of creation. Those deities are born without procreating (unlike the later gods).

The Zokasanshin (three deities of creation) are Ame-no-minaka-nushi (Central Master), Takamimusubi (High Creator) and Kamimusubi (Divine Creator). Later came Umashiashikabihikoji (Energy) and Amenotokotachi (Heaven).

The seventh and final generation of the Kamiyonanayo are the brother and sister pair, Izanagi and Izanami, the makers who form the basis of all creation. The couple were in heaven and wondered what lay below; they thrust down a spear from heaven and stirred the sea. As they lifted the spear, the liquid started dropping from the tip and this was how the first islands were created. The deities then descend to the islands and built a land. Izanagi (male) and Izanami (female) personify the Chinese principles of *yin* and *yang*.

When Izanagi and Izanami are to be married they walk from different directions to meet each other (as was the custom) and when they meet, the goddess Izanami exclaims, 'What a pleasure to meet such a handsome young man!' Afterwards, when she gives birth to a deformed child they consult the gods, who say that it had happened because Izanami had spoken first during the wedding ceremony. They have to perform the ceremony again, walking from different directions, and this time the goddess lets her husband speak first.

The pair go on to give birth to many islands, including those that constitute Japan, as well as many gods, including the gods of wind, trees and mountains. The Shinto fire god, Kagutsuchi, is their last-born son, but his fiery birth results in his mother's death. As she lies dying, her vomit, urine and excrement gives birth to other gods. Her husband's tears create the goddess Moaning-river. He is so distraught that he cuts off the head of the baby who has caused his wife's death, and drops of blood from the sword give birth to eight more gods.

Fujin, the 'God of Wind' from the Shinto religion, a terrifying wizard-like demon carrying a large bag of winds on his shoulders.

Izanami and Izanagi creating the Japanese islands.

THE ISLAND OF CREATION
EGYPT

Creation myths that arise from Egypt differ widely depending on location, but each has a primordial mound at its centre, known as the 'Island of Creation'.

Relief depicting the goddess Tefnut and the god Ptah from the Ramesseum, the memorial temple of Pharaoh Ramesses II in the Theban necropolis near present-day Luxor, Egypt.

CREATION MYTHS

In most of the myths, the world emerges from an infinite, lifeless sea, in a distant period when the sun rose for the first time. There is the presence of an eye – the sun – that creates those mounds from the chaos of the surrounding waters. The primeval hills are said to represent the fertile mounds left by the receding Nile after annual floods, and the great pyramids were built to represent the mounds.

From the dawn of time, the great goddess called Nun reigns supreme and she creates the world out of herself. She gives birth to Atum who then creates the universe. Atum is neither male nor female, and was all alone in the world. Eventually, by joining with its own shadow, Atum produces a son and a daughter. The son, Shu, is born by being spat out and becomes the god of the air. The daughter, Tefnut, is vomited out of Atum and becomes the goddess of mist and moisture. Shu and Tefnut are responsible for bringing order and stability to the chaos of the world. They produce Geb and Nut – the earth and the sky – who are at first tangled together.

Shu, the god of the air, separates his children Nut and Geb by pushing Nut into the air where she will remain arched over Geb. They long to be together but must remain apart. Nut produces rain and Geb makes things grow on earth. Therefore, the waters of chaos have been separated into the sky, the earth, and the underworld.

Shu and Tefnut produce the other gods, but they encounter misfortune. They get lost in the dark seas. Their father Atum is distraught. When they are found and returned, he weeps tears of joy and, when those tears hit the earth, they become the first humans.

In ancient Egyptian mythology we understand a familiar concept of sky and earth, but here it is in reverse: instead of sky being male and earth female, we have sky goddess Nut and her brother/husband Geb, the earth god.

It is through the Pyramid Texts – decorations and writings on tomb walls dating back to 2500BC – that we have gained most of our information regarding Egyptian creation myths.

The Goddess Nut raising the sun, from the reverse of the lid of the Djedhor sarcophagus, c.378–341BC.

The Island of Creation

Marduk: the killing of the goddess
Mesopotamia

Mesopotamia was an ancient region located near the Zagros mountains that includes today's Iraq as well as parts of Iran, Turkey and Syria. The name comes from the Greek and means 'between two rivers,' referring to the Tigris and the Euphrates. Some core gods are constant and universal, including Marduk. As with many creation myths, the details vary between different locations and tribes.

In the beginning there is only the male Apsu (fresh water) and the female Tiamat (salt water). When those two seas mingle, they create the gods Lahmu and Lahamu. The gods then produce the gods Anshar, Kishnar and Anu. From this generation of gods come Ea and his many brothers.

Ea and his brothers are restless and cause chaos and noise, so Apsu decides to destroy Ea. When Ea hears of the plan he kills Apsu first, which starts a war between the gods. Tiamat creates some monstrous creatures like the viper and the lion, led by a chief called Kingu, to go into heaven and fight Ea and his brothers. Meanwhile, Ea and the goddess Damkina create the great god Marduk. He is fearless and agrees to fight for Ea.

Marduk overcomes the monstrous Tiamat (a personification of chaos) and her army to establish order and human society. Marduk defeats Tiamat using the wind and splits her corpse into two parts that become the earth and the sky; her breasts become mountains. Marduk becomes the undisputed leader and creates the days of the year, the planets, the moon and the stars. He himself becomes the sun.

After a while he creates a being who can worship the gods while taking care of things on earth. Marduk creates a structure out of the bones left from the

Marduk sets forth to attack Tiamat.

CREATION MYTHS

dead monsters in the war, breathes life into it and leaves those first humans on earth while the gods ascend to heaven.

Tiamat is often said to represent female principle, while victorious Marduk represents the set of male attributes. Marduk becomes the first king and his kingdom is called Babylon. His temple serves as the model for the tower of Babel, and he is referred to as 'Bel' ('Lord'). Marduk's symbol animal is a snake-dragon.

The historic city of Babylon in modern-day Iraq.

THE COSMIC EGG
FINLAND

The 'world egg' – or 'cosmic egg' – is a mythological motif found in many creation myths, including Finnish mythology. Until the Kalevala, the epic poem of the 19th century, this tradition was an oral one.

In the beginning there are only the waters and the sky. Sky's daughter, Ilmater, is bored and lonely and goes down to the waters to rest. She floats there for 700 years, longing for some company. Then one day, as she is floating in the water with her knee raised, she notices a beautiful bird looking for a place to lay its eggs. Ilmater raises her knee further; the bird lands, builds a nest and lays some eggs. The bird sits on her nest warming the eggs, but also warming Ilmater's knee. The heat gets too

The Aulanko nature reserve park in Finland. According to mythology, the land was formed from the broken shell of a cosmic egg.

much and Ilmater drops her knee into the water to cool it down. This dislodges the eggs and they fall into the water where they are smashed by the waves.

From one of the eggs the creation begins. The lower part of the eggshell becomes the land, the white of the egg makes the moon and stars, and the yolk becomes the sun. After several hundred more years of floating, Ilmater begins to act on her urge to create, making beaches with her arms and pools with her footprints. Ilmater has a son, Väinämöinen, whose father is the sea, and he is the first man in the world. He does not begin as a baby, but as a wise old man with a long white beard as he has been in his mother's womb for 730 years. He swims to land and, with the help of the Great Bear in the sky, scatters seeds and creates the first flora.

Väinämöinen is an important hero in Finnish mythology: a seer who can perform magic with the songs he sings. He fights many battles, including against his main rival, the witch Louhi, a goddess of the underworld.

The details of this creation myth are recorded in the 19th-century work of epic poetry the Kalevala, compiled by Elias Lönnrot. Depending on the version, the bird is sometimes a duck, sometimes a teal, and sometimes an eagle.

One egg's lower half transformed
And became the earth below,
And its upper half transmuted
And became the sky above;
From the yolk the sun was made,
Light of day to shine upon us;
From the white the moon was formed,
Light of night to gleam above us;
All the coloured brighter bits
Rose to be the stars of heaven
And the darker crumbs changed into
Clouds and cloudlets in the sky.
– Kalevala

To this day there is an annual feast day in Finland on the 26th of August to honour and celebrate Ilmater.

Statue of Väinämöinen, Ilmater's son and the Finnish and Karelian hero, in Monrepo park, Russia.

The song of the birth of the world
Estonia

Estonia is a small country with a long history, and song is at its centre. Despite its small population it has managed to create hundreds of thousands of different folksongs.

The beautiful Estonian landscape is the setting of hundreds of thousands of different folksongs and myths.

In an Estonian song about the birth of the world a bird lays three eggs and when they hatch, one becomes the sun, one becomes the moon and the third becomes the earth. Typically, the bird flies over water in search of somewhere to nest; she lays three eggs that are swept into the water and then emerge as the sun, the moon and the earth. In other versions the bird flies over bushes, usually three, and spurns two in favour of the third.

Kalevipoeg, the hero of the Estonian national epic, Kalevipoeg carrying planks of wood which he characteristically hurls at his enemies.

In some versions the bird is a swallow, but often her species is not designated, and instead she is referred to as 'pretty bird' or 'little bird'. She usually has blue plumage in these tales.

While details of Estonian mythology are scattered throughout historical chronicles, the folklore was not recorded in a systematic way until the 19th-century. Some traces of the oldest myths have survived in runic folk ballads that cover topics as broad as work, lamentations and epic legends.

Loomislaul ('of creation') is an Estonian folk song about creation that has many different versions all over the country. *Loomislaul* is acted out with participants who accompany the singing, playing the parts of the bird, its eggs and the nestlings. The older and more archaic melody is typical of northern Estonia, whereas the more modern, rhymed song and dance is associated with southern Estonia.

The song of the birth of the world

The lands pulled up from the sea by a giant fish hook   Polynesia

The story of Maui, a great hero of Polynesian mythology, begins when he is a premature baby who is cast aside by his mother. She wraps him in her hair and places him in the ocean. The ocean takes care of him and gives him special shape-shifting powers. He returns to his village as a young man and seeks out his mother and brothers. Maui has magical powers and so is much stronger than his four brothers.

Maui makes a fish hook from his grandmother's jawbone with which he snares the sun. He uses the bone to beat the sun so that when it returns to the sky it will slow down, allowing more time for his people to work.

One day his four brothers plan a fishing trip, but they don't tell Maui because they don't want him to come. However, early the next morning he hides away in his brothers' canoe. The brothers set off in high spirits. When they find a good place to fish they stop paddling. But Maui surprises them by jumping out of his hiding place and insists that they keep paddling. Soon it begins to get dark and they lose sight of the land. His brothers fall asleep one by one but Maui keeps paddling all night. In the morning, Maui is happy because he has found a fishing place he is satisfied with. But his brothers are tired and grumpy and in their anger they refuse to give him any bait to fish with.

Instead he strikes his own face with the jawbone fish hook he'd made, causing a nosebleed, and he uses the blood as bait. He flings his special hook into the ocean where it sinks to the depths. His hook snares something. He starts to pull and pull, finding the object much heavier and tougher to pull in than a normal fish.

Maui uses every muscle in his body to pull in the fishing line, chanting magical incantations (*karakia*) as he does so, and feels something begin to stir under the ocean. His brothers make no move to help as the sea churns and the boat rocks.

New Zealand's Urapukapuka Island in the Bay of Islands.

Maui, the legendary hero of New Zealand. Descended from the gods, he was a fisherman who used a magic jawbone for fishing and caught and pulled New Zealand out of the sea.

> The Maori names for New Zealand's North and South Islands are *Te Ika-a-Maui* ('the fish of Maui') and *Te Waka-a-Maui* ('the canoe of Maui'). Maui had stood on the latter while pulling the former out of the ocean.

Finally, Maui pulls a huge fish to the surface; its tail stretches far to the north and its head lies far in the south. Maui wants to retrieve his hook and so leaves his brothers standing on the fish, telling them not to touch it.

However, as soon as Maui is gone, the brothers start hacking away at the catch to claim some of the fish for themselves. The fish writhes in agony and before long its once smooth back is covered in valleys and ranges. In time Maui's fish becomes the rugged landmass of New Zealand's North Island and his canoe becomes the South Island.

Maui is also a renowned trickster, known for his ingenuity and creativity. Maui tricks Mahuika, Goddess of Fire, and steals the fire to give it to mankind.

He desires immortality for humans and thinks this can be achieved by killing Hine Nui Te Po, the Goddess of Death. Maui transforms himself into a snake and wriggles inside her vagina, but she is awoken by a flock of noisy birds and kills Maui by crushing him inside her.

The lands pulled up from the sea by a giant fish hook

The Vedic creation myth
India

The Vedic period in Indian mythology is also referred to as ancient Hinduism and Brahmanism. Scholars have dated the earliest surviving Indian myths to around 4000BC.

Agni, the Vedic fire god of Hinduism.

Sacred texts from the Indian sub-continent, including the *Rig Veda*, the *Puranas*, the *Mahabharata* and the *Ramayana*, provide variations on the same foundational stories. Every Indian myth contains a poetic sense and openness to interpretation that is rare in world mythology. Metaphor is a constant theme found in the narratives in these texts.

The foundational stories include the earth as a universal mother, that creation and destruction are erstwhile companions, and that meditation is a way to accumulate power (and thus that intellectual strength equals or surpasses physical energy). Time is represented as a continuum in which past, present and future are the same thing and the only certainty is that the same events will recur again and again.

The oldest creation myths can be found in the *Rig Veda* collection of hymns. This is the first of four Vedas composed by Aryan invaders that forms the basis for Vedism.

The mythological motif of the cosmic egg is also found in the Vedic creation myth. In the beginning the waters are vast and deep and everything in existence is nonbeing. The waters produce a golden egg that floats for nine months. After this time, the egg bursts open and Prajapati appears standing in the shell. Prajapati is neither male nor female, but a powerful combination of both. Prajapati rests on the egg for a year without moving or speaking. After a year, Prajapati breaks the silence and the first word spoken becomes the earth. The next word becomes the sky, which is divided into seasons.

Prajapati can see his future, a life unrolling before him for a thousand years until his death. This makes Prajapati feel lonely and he divides into two beings, a husband and a wife, who together create the gods and mankind.

First born is Agni, the god of fire, and many other gods soon follow, both good and evil. Prajapati separates the good and evil gods, and banishes the evil offspring deep into the earth.

Over time, Prajapati's beautiful daughter Dawn grows up to be a highly desirable woman. One day, when she is roaming the earth in the form of a doe, Prajapati adopts the form of a stag and rapes her. From this unwanted union she gives birth to all the cattle of the world. The other gods watch in horror; they can't believe Prajapati's disgraceful behaviour. In response they create the monstrous Rudra who hunts Prajapati across the earth. When Rudra finds Prajapati, still in stag form, he shoots him into the sky with an arrow. Prajapati becomes the 'Deer's Head' (or Capricorn) constellation in the night sky.

In post-Vedic Hinduism, Prajapati has been identified with the god Brahma.

Hindu deities in Kapaleeshwarar Temple, Chennai, India

The Vedic creation myth

THE CREATIVE SACRIFICE
CHINA AND INDONESIA

In Chinese and Indonesian myths, a common theme is the sacrifice of super-human divinities whose bodies become part of the natural world. In the South Pacific regions of the world, these beings are known as dema deities. In many traditions their bodies also bestow practical items, edible plants to feed people, as well as rituals and knowledge.

PAN-GU/PAN-KU

According to Chinese myth, at the beginning of the world there was no difference between sky and land, heaven and earth. All is contained in an egg-shape, a cosmic black egg that carries all the chaos but also contains a balance of yin and yang. The first human, Pan-Gu, inhabits this space and lies alone sleeping for eighteen thousand years. When he wakes he stretches and breaks the membrane, releasing all of the parts of the universe. This is how the sky and earth are made.

After all of this time sleeping, Pan-Gu has grown to be a giant. Noticing chaos has ended he decides to make order a permanent arrangement by holding apart the sky and the earth with his huge body. He spends a further eighteen thousand years in this position and all remains intact. After this time has elapsed, he dies. Each part of his body is forms as features of the earth and sky: his limbs mark out a compass and mountain ranges; his blood becomes waterways; his teeth and his bones form the earth's minerals and rocks. His eyes become the sun and the moon. His death adds features to the universe and follows his form.

There are many varieties of Pan-Gu's physical appearance in the different myths from across China: sometimes he has a dog's head and a man's body; in some he is very short. There are versions where he is assisted by a turtle, a qilin, a phoenix and a dragon. There is also a variation where parasites on his body create the first humans.

A depiction of Pan-Gu and the beginning of the universe composed of Yin and Yang. Yang formed the sky and Yin condensed to become the Earth.

A Kecak dance performed by many male dancers in Bali. According to myth, Hainuwele was attacked and killed during a traditional dance performed by the male members of her tribe.

Hainuwele and the origin of crops

In West Seram, South West Pacific, Ameta is the first man to discover the coconut. He receives instructions in a dream teaching him how to plant it. In three days, a very high tree has grown. Ameta climbs the tree to harvest its flowers and, in so doing, he cuts himself and spills his blood on a blossom. In three more days, he finds a girl has grown from this branch. The girl, Hainuwele, has the extraordinary power to defecate very valuable objects. Despite her generosity, the men of the tribe become jealous and attack her, burying her alive and dispersing her objects of wealth.

When Ameta discovers her body he cuts it up and plants each piece in a separate place, which causes tubers to grow. These become food for the people. After these events, the divine leader Mulua Satene, disgusted at the first act of killing in her community, announces her departure. Before she leaves she forces each man to cross a threshold where they become animals or ghosts, or remain as men. There are many complexities to this myth relating to how society works: involving money, defilement, and power, and a strict order of patterned numbers.

This myth was first recorded by an anthropologist in the early 20th-century and it is contested as to whether it is an ancient myth or a more recent reconstruction of legend to explain socioeconomic conflict. Nonetheless, it captures the anxieties of a society moving from hunter-gatherers to domiciled plant-growers, and provides an insight into relations between men and women when such change occurs.

The creative sacrifice

The Aztec creation myth
Mexico

Unlike some creation myths, the Aztec story is not one of endless cycles but has a clear beginning. It originates in ancient Mexico and the surrounding areas and, as with many myths, it has evolved over time. It is a story of birth, death and rebirth: when the world is destroyed, it is reborn, along with a new sun, through the sacrifice of one of the gods. The legend of the five suns tells us that five worlds, and therefore five suns, have existed.

In the beginning there is a void. Then the dual god Ometechuhtli creates itself: it is both male and female, good and evil, chaos and order. Being both male and female, Ometechuhtli can produce children, and gives birth to four: Xipe Totec (north), Quetzalcoatl (east), Huizilopochtli (south) and Tezcatlipoca (west). Directions were very important to the Aztecs, as they believed their great empire to be at the centre of the universe.

These four gods create water and other gods, but they also create the sea monster Cipactli, part fish, part crocodile. This monster is huge and devours all. The four gods decide to go to war with Cipactli. They attack and defeat the monster by pulling it in four directions. This is how the universe is created.

There is another version of the myth. At the beginning of time, there is only the earth mother Coatlicue, swimming in the vast and treacherous waters. She creates the moon, the sun and the stars, and then she has a daughter, the earth goddess Coyolxauhqui. Her daughter and other children ascend to the sky.

One day Coatlicue finds a ball of feathers and tucks them inside her dress. The feathers impregnate her and when her children in heaven discover what has happened they are furious. They don't believe her story and decide to kill her for the shame she has brought on the family. As she is

A statue of Coatlicue displayed in the National Anthropology Museum in Mexico City.

Mictlantecuhtli (left), god of death, the lord of the underworld, and Quetzalcoatl (right), god of wisdom, life, knowledge, morning star, patron of the winds and light and the lord of the West. Together they symbolize life and death.

being chased, she hears the voice of her unborn child saying he is ready. She gives birth to a fully armed and fiery sun god, Huitzilopochtil. With one swing of his fiery sword, he cuts the earth goddess Coyolxauhqui in half and sends her body in two directions; the top half goes into the sky and becomes the heavens, while the bottom half crashes towards the sea and becomes the earth.

Huitzilopochtil ascends to the heavens while his mother Coatlicue stays on earth. Another son, Quetzalcoatl, the feathered serpent, creates the first humans from ash. At first the earth provides everything that this new race of men needs – they are safe, free from disease, and food is plentiful. But they become greedy, start taking the earth for granted, and stop honouring the gods. Quetzalcoatl is furious and decides to wash away all the humans in a flood.

There are only two non-greedy humans, husband and wife Teta and Nena, and Quetzalcoatl decides to spare them. They go on to repopulate the world with a new and more humble race. But Coatlicue is not as generous as before and with an insatiable hunger for human blood she demands one human heart a year, in exchange for maintaining the earth's riches.

The Aztec creation myth

The universality of 'the serpent'
World mythologies

Serpents appear in almost every mythology in the world. They are often thought to hypnotize their prey or cast a spell on them. Humans have been attracted to and repelled by these creatures from earliest times. The myths are mainly associated with their venom and a perceived ability to strike by surprise in a range of guises. Serpents in mythology include the snake with its tail in its mouth, the ouroboros (or uroboros); this is an ancient symbol of eternity dating from ancient times. In ancient Egypt the serpent was regarded as a symbol of immortality and also of death; the pharaoh wore a snake emblem on his headdress as a mark of royalty and divinity.

The snake plays an important role in the Biblical story of the Garden of Eden, home to the first humans – Adam and Eve. Here the snake persuades Eve to eat the fruit of the tree of knowledge of good and evil – even though God has forbidden her from doing so. The serpent has therefore corrupted Eve with knowledge and wisdom. This brings about the expulsion of Adam and Eve from the garden and introduces the concept of mortality to the first humans.

Dreamtime Serpent near Birdsville and Betoota, outback Queensland, Australia; a work of art representing pathways travelled through country to connect the river systems.

CREATION MYTHS

Serpents are identified as immortal in this world through the act of shedding their skins – the newly emerging snake representing rebirth. They are regarded as living to a great age and therefore knowing the earth intimately, which implies that they must possess great wisdom. In the New Testament, Jesus Christ calls on his followers to be as 'wise as serpents' (Matthew 10.16). In the *Epic of Gilgamesh* (see page 176), a snake snatches the plant of immortality from Gilgamesh and eats it, and then sheds its skin.

Nearly every culture has a legend of a serpent, often wise, that rules the earth. In many myths, snakes are said to have arrived from the sky, including Quetzalcoatl, the feathered serpent of the Aztecs, who descends from heaven in a silver egg.

Many indigenous people, including Australian Aborigines, venerate a Rainbow Serpent. This also appears in the mythology of some African tribes, where it is called Aido Hwendo and is believed to support the earth.

The serpent is evident across the whole field of Greek mythology. The head of snakes made Medusa, one of the Gorgons, especially terrifying to all who encountered her. The amphisbaena is a mythological snake with a head at both ends, making it duplicitous and very dangerous. In a speech by Cassandra in Aeschylus' play *Agamemnon*, she names Clytemnestra an amphisbaena to indicate her treachery.

The ability to shed its skin has given rise to the belief that snakes have the power to heal; a serpent coiled round a staff (the Rod of Asclepius) is the symbol adopted by doctors of medicine. Asclepius, the god of medicine, brought the dead back to life and was killed for this crime against nature by Zeus, who struck him with a thunderbolt. The figure of the twin serpent winding around the staff of Asclepius is sometimes confused with the Caduceus, the staff of the god Hermes, which is winged and has two serpents coiled around it. It represents Hermes, the messenger of the gods, who guides the dead to the underworld and protects merchants, shepherds, gamblers, liars and thieves.

The Caduceus symbol depicting a herald's wand with two serpents entwined around it. In Greek and Roman mythology it was carried by the messenger gods Hermes and Mercury.

The universality of 'the serpent'

Men as birds and women as fish
Korea

In early Korean mythology, men are equated with birds and women with fish. Tales concerning women often have links to the sea or water, whereas men have links to the sky, wind and rain. This is a variation on the common sky father/earth mother theme. These themes are detailed in the Samguk Yusa (Memorabilia of the Three Kingdoms), a collection of legends and folklores relating to the three kingdoms of Korea (Goguryeo, Baekje and Silla). The earliest copy of this text was written in classical Chinese in the 1280s.

According to legend, nine elders rule an area in the south of Korea, but there is no king. One day a voice speaks from heaven and directs the people to an area/mountain called Kuji. Several hundred people gather there, including two of the elders. The voice instructs them to go to the top of the mountain, dig some earth, do a dance and sing a song (now known as *Kujiga*). As they do this, a gold chest descends from heaven on the end of a cord. They open the chest and discover six golden orbs. They close the chest and take it to the home of the elders. Next morning, when they look inside it again, the orbs have transformed into a baby boy.

This baby, who is called Suro (also Kim Suro or So-Roo), grows quickly and soon reaches 2.7m (9ft) tall. He comes to rule an area called Kaya, where he builds a palace. The nine elders encourage him to take a bride, but he refuses, saying heaven will take care of him. Heo Hwang Ok, a 16-year-old princess from India, arrives by boat and he marries her. Her parents had previously had a dream that their daughter would marry the king, so they send her to meet her fate. She lives as queen until the age of 157.

Suro transforms into a bird. His wife does not transform into a fish, but is connected to water because of her arrival by sea.

Samguk Yusa (Memorabilia of the Three Kingdoms) displayed in Seoul National University. The earliest version of the text is believed to have been compiled in the 1280s, and the earliest extant publication of the text is from 1512.

> The mythological beliefs of the Koreans have been deeply influenced by Buddhism and Chinese mythology, as well as indigenous Korean shamanistic beliefs. Animism (see page 230) is a dominant aspect of Korean mythology, particularly in the worshipping of mountains and creatures such as snakes.

CREATION MYTHS

Envoys from the Three Kingdoms of Korea: Baekje, Goguryeo and Silla.

Sky god and water nymph

Goddess Yuhwa is a water nymph, daughter of the river god, and Haemosu is a sky god who wears a crown of crow feathers. Haemosu desires Yuhwa so he builds a copper palace in which to trap her. Yuhwa and her sisters – intrigued by the sudden appearance of the palace – go inside to explore. The attendants try to bolt the doors but two of the sisters escape. Yuhwa, however, is trapped and is taken away to be Haemosu's wife.

The origin of fire and light
World Mythologies

The discovery and control of fire is a crucial milestone in human development, as much for the warmth, comfort and security it brings as for its importance in cooking food. There are many variations in Native American folklore regarding the origin of fire.

According to a Mi'kmaq legend, the demigod Kluskap (also known as Glooskap) meets a wise old woman called Nukumi. Kluskap says he wants to learn from her. Nukumi offers to act like a grandmother for him and share her wisdom, but she can no longer survive on a diet of plants and berries. Kluskap enlists the help of his animal friends and asks a robin to fly to a place where lightning has hit the ground and to bring him back the sparks. The robin uses two sticks to transport the sparks because they are too hot to hold. As the robin flies, the wind blows the sparks and the robin's breast turns red. Still, he succeeds in taking the fire to Kluskap and Nukumi, who then use it to cook. To this day, fire is created from the sparks of two sticks rubbed together, and all robins' breasts are red.

A photograph of the Mi'kmaq people from 1865.

A dance from The Mi'kmaq Legends, *a modern performance based on traditional stories.*

CREATION MYTHS

Prometheus and the gift of fire

In Greek mythology, the Titan-god Prometheus steals fire for the people and hides it in a reed, which provokes the wrath of Zeus, his cousin. Some myths credit Prometheus as being the creator of man, and he is often seen animating his creations with fire. It is said that he created the first men from potter's clay, with two legs to mirror the gods.

Prometheus is known as the god of forethought, the bringer of fire, and a friend of mortals. For this act of giving fire to mankind, Prometheus is seen as a significant cultural figure. Before this, fire had been for the use of the gods alone.

Zeus punishes Prometheus by having him chained to a rock. Every day his liver is pecked out by an eagle and every day it grows back. Zeus swears that Prometheus will never be released, but Heracles shoots the eagle and frees Prometheus. Nevertheless, Zeus forces Prometheus to wear one of the links of the chain that held him captive to the rock as a ring around his finger.

Prometheus is a prophet who can foresee the future. When Zeus plans to send a great flood to earth to destroy the human race, Prometheus foresees it and warns his son Deucalion so that he can escape.

Prometheus Bound (c.1640-1645) by Jacob Jordaens, depicting the Titan's eternal punishment.

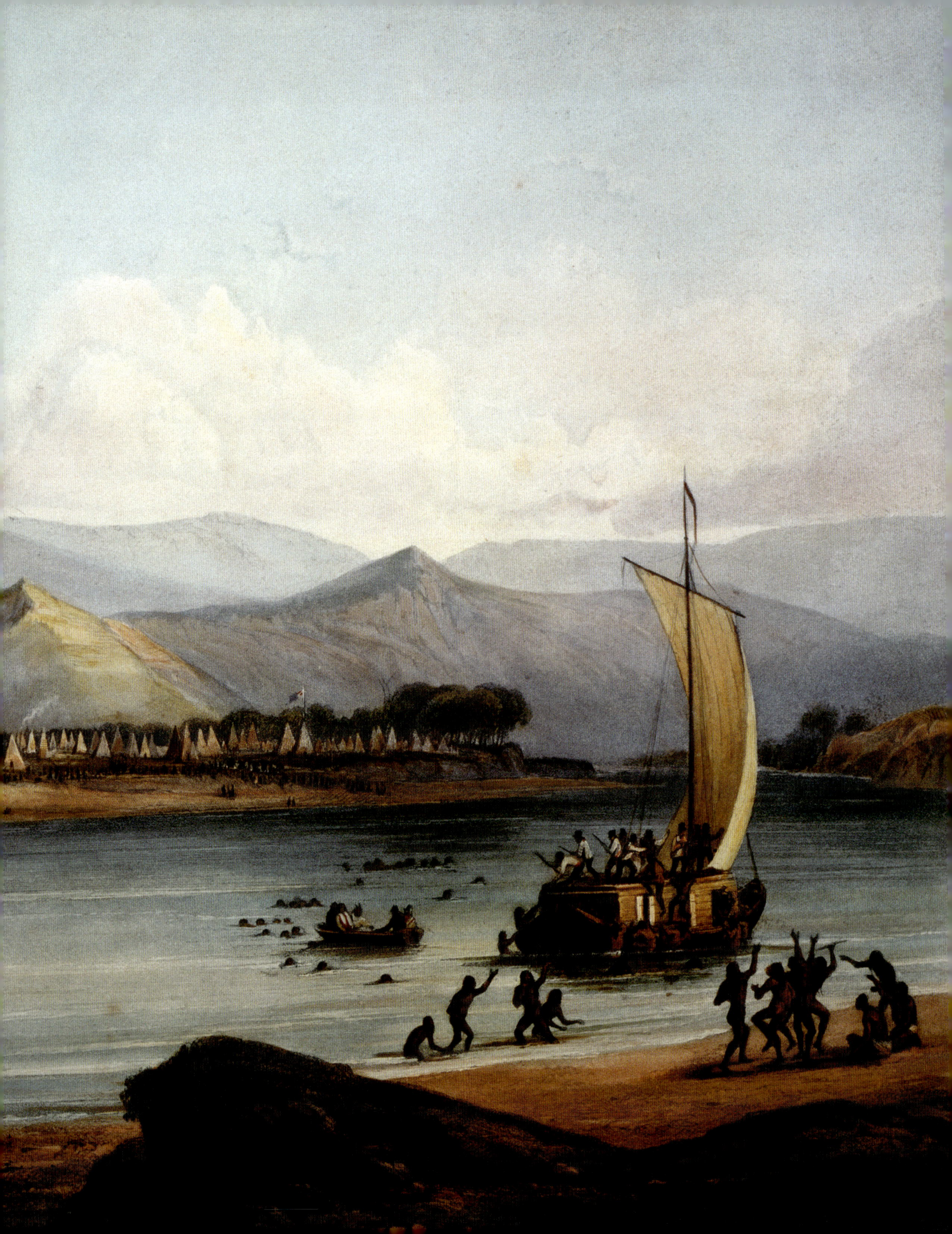

GREAT FLOODS

Humans have always been at the mercy of powerful acts of nature such as floods. These catastrophic events are often explained as interventions by the gods, usually as punishment. The cataclysmic flood is sometimes described as a move by the gods to destroy the human race so as to start again, as with the story of Noah.

Noah and the Ark
Middle East

The story of Noah's Ark is found in the Bible's Book of Genesis. Many believe the Ark actually existed and came to rest on Mount Ararat in Turkey.

A long time has passed since Adam and Eve were created, and God is now very unhappy because the world is full of wicked people. There is only one good, law-abiding man, and his name is Noah. God blesses Noah and tells him that he plans to destroy all the evil people in the world, but he wants to save Noah and his family. He asks Noah to build a huge boat, called an ark, and load his family on to it, along with two of every species of animal: one male and one female. God plans to send rain for forty days and forty nights until the earth is flooded. Only Noah, his family and the animals he houses on the boat will survive.

Noah's Ark as depicted in the 12th-century Romanesque frescoes in the Abbey Church of Saint-Savin-sur-Gartempe, France.

The Entry of the Animals into Noah's Ark, by Jan Brueghel the Elder, painted in 1613. Animals fill the earth and sky as they are shepherded by Noah towards the ark in the far distance.

Noah does everything that God asks for. He spends many days building the Ark, and then loads his family and the animals on to it, along with enough food to last for a long time.

As promised, God sends the rain for forty days and forty nights, and Noah, his family and the animals on the ark are safe. When the rain finally stops, Noah sends a dove out every day to find land. The dove keeps coming back with nothing, but finally returns with an olive leaf in its beak. This indicates to Noah that the earth is starting to dry out and he will be able to find land.

The Ark comes to rest on Mount Ararat. Noah and his family step off the boat after a year and are very happy to have survived the flood. God is also happy because all the evil has been washed away. Noah goes on to repopulate the earth with good people, who have God in their hearts.

The tree god myth
Korea

There are several flood myths in Korean mythology, influenced by Korean shamanistic religion, Chinese mythology and Buddhism. The Namu Doryeong, or Namu Toryong (A Son of the Tree God) myth, is the best known. A young boy, Namu Doryeong, the son of a fairy and a laurel tree, is a free spirit who wanders the bush. Heavy rains come and the land is flooded, but Namu Doryeong survives the flood by floating on his laurel tree. He tries to save some animals, starting with the smallest – ants and mosquitoes – and lets them rest on his tree. He also rescues another small boy.

The tree finally comes to rest on the top of the highest mountain in Korea, Baekdu-san, where Namu Doryeong finds other survivors: a wise old woman, her daughter and her foster daughter. The old woman wants her natural daughter to marry the cleverer of the two boys and so she sets a test. Whoever is the fastest at gathering grain from the sand will win her daughter's hand. Namu Doryeong is helped by the ants he saved and so wins.

When the wise old woman realizes he has had help, she declares the issue will be decided by chance. She locks the two girls in dark rooms and says that the boys can choose a room. This time the mosquitoes that Namu Doryeong saved help him by flying into the rooms and telling him which daughter is in each room.

So, Namu Doryeong marries the old woman's daughter and the other boy marries the foster daughter and they repopulate the world.

Thanks to this myth, Baekdu-san, a semi-active volcano, has become an intrinsic part of Korean identity and pride. The mountain is still considered a holy place by both North and South Koreans, and by the Chinese whose country it borders.

*The Camphor laurel (*Cinnamomum camphora*) tree, native to Korea. Namu Doryeong avoids drowning by clinging to a floating laurel tree such as this. The tree eventually brings him to the mountain Baekdu-san where he meets the other survivors of the flood.*

Located on the border of China and North Korea, Mount Baekdu (or Mount Paektu) is an active volcano that overlooks the crater of Heaven Lake. To the North Koreans it is known as Paekdu-san, but to the South Koreans it is known as Baekdu-san. It is still revered by both countries as the spiritual home of Korea.

The tree god myth

Nanabozho and the Great Serpent
North America

Native American flooding stories are plentiful and varied, particularly among the Algonquian-speaking tribes of North America. One famous story concerns Nanabozho and the Great Serpent. Nanabozho is also known by other names including Nanabush and Tcakabesh (among the eastern Algonquian peoples from north of the Abenaki areas).

According to Ojibwe legend, Nanabozho, son of the West Wind, returns home one day to find his cousin is missing. He sees snake tracks and follows them to the edge of a lake. When he looks down into the lake, he sees the lair of the Great Serpent and the evil spirits. The Great Serpent has killed Nanabozho's cousin and the body can be seen under the water. Taking his revenge, Nanabozho fires an arrow at the Great Serpent, but before the serpent finally dies, the creature uses his evil spirits to cause a great flood. Nanabozho flees the angry waters and warns the people in his village, who had gathered at the top of a mountain. Soon all the earth and all the mountains, apart from the one on which Nanabozho stands, are under water. Nanabozho builds a raft out of timber and saves some humans and animals. The last mountain soon disappears under the water. When the water finally subsides, the people learn that the Great Serpent is dead and it is safe for them to return.

Ouimet Canyon Provincial Park, in Thunder Bay, Ontario, the setting of the great flood and Nanabozho's conflict with the Great Serpent.

The Creator's pipe
North America

According to the legends of the A'ani (also known as A'aninin, Haaninin, Atsina and Gros Ventre), an Algonquian-speaking Plains tribe located in north central Montana, the Creator is disappointed in the wild people of the world and how they live, so he decides to make a new world.

He takes a long pipe and attaches sticks and dried buffalo dung to it, to ensure it will float. Then he sings three times, shouts three times and kicks the earth. The earth cracks and water floods the earth. After floating alone on his pipe for a time, the Creator unwraps the animals that are kept in his pipe. He sends a turtle under water to see if it can find land. The turtle returns with some mud and the Creator uses it to make land, and then creates many humans and animals from earth. He promises them that if they behave well, the world will not flood again, and shows them a rainbow as a sign the rain has gone.

A 19th-century depiction of a A'ani campsite along the Missouri River by Karl Bodmer.

The Great Flood and Yu the Great

China

Chinese mythology developed out of the country's three main religions – Buddhism, Taoism and Confucianism.

Wang village/Furong zhen in Hunan province, China.

Yu is an ancient hero in Chinese mythology – called 'Dayu' in Chinese, with 'Yu' being his name and 'Da' meaning 'great'. Yu the Great is best known for controlling floods. The Great Flood of Gun-Yu (also known as the Great Flood of China or the Gun-Yu myth) is a major flood that has lasted at least two generations and caused widespread disaster and the displacement of the Chinese people.

Gun (Yu's father) has been working on a solution to control the flood for nearly a decade, but his efforts aren't working. His son, Yu, takes over and comes up with a new solution: digging channels to conduct water to the sea, which work much more effectively. Yu the Great is also credited with introducing agriculture to the people, allowing them to fully utilize water and soil under his control. He teaches people how to breed ducks, geese and fish, and allows his son to teach people how to plant rice and other crops.

Yu leaves his home just four days after his marriage to go and control the waters. His son is born, but he doesn't return to his house for thirteen years, putting the needs of the people ahead of his own needs.

At that time, the people choose the ruler. Yu the Great is supported by the people and taken over from Shun. In 2070BC, Yu establishes the Xia dynasty and opens a new era in Chinese history. His son, Qi of Xia, succeeds him and so begins a new tradition of dynastic succession.

There is no evidence Yu actually existed, and some argue that he was more of a god or mythical animal than a real person. Some versions of the myth tell of Yu being assisted by mythical beasts such as a channel-digging dragon and a mud-hauling turtle.

A map of the Yellow River area was given to Yu by either Houtu (the goddess queen of the earth) or Hebo (the god of the Yellow River).

King Yu, from a painting of a hanging scroll in the National Palace Museum, Taipei.

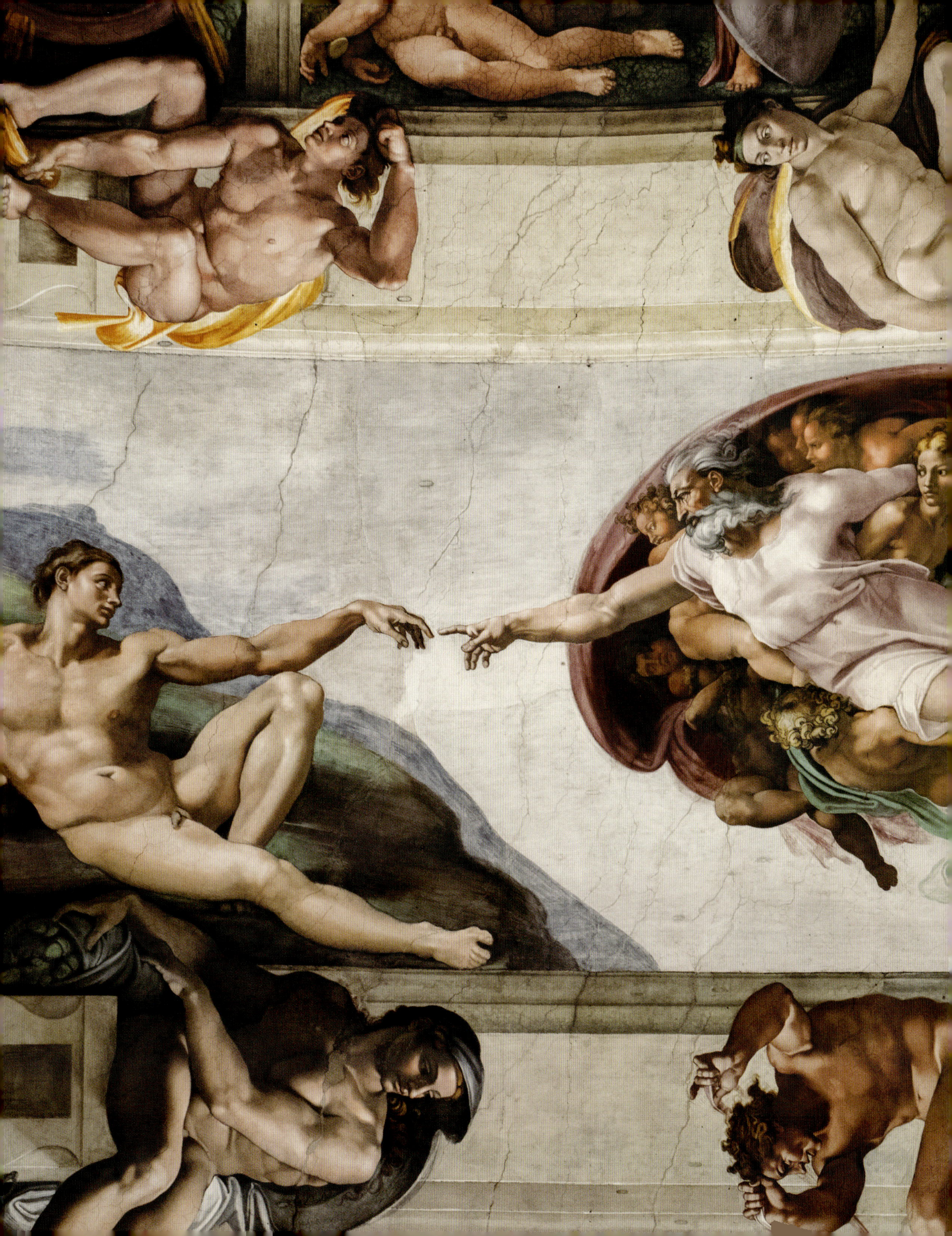

Cosmology

In the next set of examples, you'll read of the variety of myths of the world and how they evolved. When ancient humans developed language, they began to explore their world with an enhanced sense of play. This narrative ability is the reason we have such a rich tradition across every part of the globe of stories and systems of belief. It served as an imaginative way to think about the cosmos and consider the key arrangements of the universe: where the stars were placed, how heaven and earth operated, and what the underworld was. Cosmology is a serious study of the universe started by our ancestors, matched by poetry and a poetic treatment of its natural phenomena and metaphysical features.

THE WORLD AS EVIL
PERSIA

Zoroastrianism is an ancient pre-Islamic religion of Persia that still survives in isolated areas of Iran and in some areas of India. Founded by the prophet Zoroaster in the 6th century BC, Zoroastrianism shares many central concepts with Christianity and Islam. It was the official religion of Persia from 600BC to AD650.

Zoroastrians believe there is one God, Ahura Mazda (the Wise Lord) who has created the world. Also known as Ohrmazd and Hourmazd, Ahura Mazda is the Avestan name for the sole God and creator. At the age of thirty, while out collecting water for a sacred ritual, Zoroaster has a revelation. He is led to the presence of Ahura Mazda and taught the cardinal principals of the 'good religion' that later becomes Zoroastrianism. Zoroaster declares Ahura Mazda to be an 'uncreated spirit'. The book of holy scriptures is called the Avesta.

The fundamental duality of Zoroastrianism is illustrated in the fact that Ahura Mazda has a twin spirit called Angra Mainyu. Ahura Mazda embodies goodness and wisdom, while Angra Mainyu embodies evil.

This dualism is a fundamental aspect of Zoroastrianism in that good and evil are regarded as being totally separate, cosmically as well as morally, to the extent that each occupies a separate sphere. Cosmic duality refers to the ongoing battle between Ahura Mazda (good) and Angra Mainyu (evil), whereas moral duality refers to the opposing forces for good and evil in the individual's mind.

Ahura Mazda has created a pure and perfect world through his creative energy. But Angra Mainyu constantly opposes this positive energy, by attacking the world with destructive energy, such as sickness, ageing and famine.

When God creates mankind, he gives all humans the gift of free will. Therefore, it is the choice of each human whether they follow good or evil. If they follow good, their path will lead to peace and everlasting happiness in heaven. If they follow evil, their path will lead to misery and eventually hell. When all mankind chooses the first option, we will have peace on earth and evil will be defeated.

A 19th-century depiction of Ahura Mazda triumphing over Angra Mainyu.

The Zoroastrian religion and sacred texts are based on this idea of a constant battle between these forces, with the belief that God and purity will eventually triumph. The presence of evil makes our world vulnerable and ever changing. The Zoroastrian scriptures urge people to take utmost care in their day-to-day lives and to live by Zoroaster's three commandments: good thoughts, good words and good deeds.

Ahura Mazda creates spirits, known as yazatas, to help him, and enlists the help of humans in his struggle against Angra Mainyu, the evil spirit who is the bringer of all misery and sin to the world. Sometimes portrayed as Ahura Mazda's twin, Angra Mainyu is understood to be inferior to Ahura Mazda. In time he will be defeated, and good will win over evil.

Angra Mainyu and his evil spirits, known as daevas, try to attract humans away from the path of righteousness and cause chaos and destruction to Ahura Mazda's perfect creation.

While Angra Mainyu is traditionally portrayed as Ahura Mazda's binary opposite, more modern versions of Zoroastrianism claim that Angra Mainyu is an emanation, derived from the first reality of a perfect God.

The Faravahar symbol at the ancient Zoroastrian Fire Temple in Yazd, Iran. The Faravahar symbolizes the basic tenets of Zorastrianism: Good thoughts, Good words and Good deeds. In modern times, it has come to be adopted as secular symbol of Iranian national identity.

The battle of good and evil
Middle East

In Christian belief, God has been involved in an epic battle with Satan, the devil, since before the time of Adam and Eve.

Before God's creation of heaven and earth, a high-ranking angel named Lucifer serves him. Lucifer persuades some of the other angels to join him in turning against God, and a great battle ensues. The beautiful earth that God has created is destroyed, and Lucifer's name is changed to Satan, which means adversary. The fallen angels who join him in the rebellion become known as demons, which means evil spirits.

Satan and his demons are punished and sent to hell, and God re-creates the earth, placing Adam and Eve in the Garden of Eden and

The Creation of Adam, *one of nine scenes from the Book of Genesis that form part of the ceiling decoration of the Sistine Chapel in the Vatican, painted by Michelangelo between 1508 and 1512*

An engraving by the German master Albrecht Dürer. Adam holds a branch from the Tree of Life, while Eve holds a branch from the forbidden Tree of Knowledge.

instructing them on how to live a good life. This includes accepting God's laws without question and living in a state of 'blissful ignorance'.

However, Satan and his demons are not yet ready to give in, and they infiltrate the Garden of Eden. Satan convinces Adam and Eve that they don't have to listen to God and that they are, in fact, free to make their own choices – the result of this is that sin and death are brought into the world.

So, as a result of Satan portraying God as a liar and an oppressor, and with the help of a wily serpent, Adam eats from the tree of knowledge and sin appears in the world. Christians believe that this deception and confusion continues to cause darkness in the world, and that people need to realize that God is the only one who can teach them how to live their lives.

The Christian Church believes there is a division between those who have chosen truth and light, and those who have chosen darkness and lies. There is some debate among Christian theologians as to whether God created the Devil. God created Lucifer, who became the Devil, but Lucifer was an angel who only became evil through his own doing. Jesus strips Satan of his authority when he is on the cross, so that Satan cannot influence people who follow Christ. The only people Satan has authority over are those who choose to believe his lies.

Satan's domain is the underworld – called 'hell' from the name of the Norse goddess of the underworld 'Hel' – but he still exerts power on earth. God cares about this influence and came to earth in the person of his son, Jesus Christ. The Bible tells how Jesus has come to lead the people on the path of righteousness again.

The battle of good and evil

YORUBA PHILOSOPHY
NIGERIA

Today's Yoruba people number approximately 43 million, predominantly in Nigeria but also in surrounding countries. There are also thriving Yoruba communities in Brazil and Cuba, descendants of the slaves transported from Africa during the 16th to 18th centuries.

The Yoruba of Nigeria have a collective noun (*itan*) that includes religion, mythology and history. Yoruba mythology is still used to resolve disputes today. The religion is often referred to as simply Itan, but is also known as Aborisha or Orisha-Ifa.

Two important Yoruba concepts are *ayanmo*, meaning human destiny or choice, and *ori*, literally meaning head and referring to intuition. The failure or success of a person is based on choices they make in heaven before birth. If a person suddenly becomes rich, it is because of good choices made before they were born. However, destiny does not come to all at the same time, so a person mustn't give up as the right life for them may not have arrived yet.

In Yoruba mythology, there is a simple distinction between *aiye*, the physical world, and *orun*, the invisible world. Nature is not an impersonal object or phenomenon, but is filled with religious significance. The world of orun is symbolized, or manifested, by visible and concrete phenomena and elements of the natural world. According to Kenyan philosopher John Mbiti, the invisible world of orun presses hard upon the visible world of aiye, and Yoruba people can 'see' orun when they look at, hear or feel the tangible world of aiye. The physical and spiritual are the two dimensions of one and the same universe.

Olodumare (also known as Eledumare) is the supreme creator in the Yoruba pantheon. He orders the first king, Oduduwa, to bring human life to earth. Oduduwa is revered as both a deity and the ancestor of the first dynasty of earthly kings. In 1969, Mbiti recorded the following five categories of spiritual and physical existence that can be observed in Yoruba culture, as well as other African societies:

1. God as the ultimate explanation of the genesis and sustenance of man and all things.
2. Spirits, made up of superhuman beings and the spirits of ancestors.
3. Man, including human beings alive and those not yet born.
4. Animals and plants or the remainders of biological life.
5. Phenomena and objects without biological life.

A brass and zinc figurine of a Yoruba King from 11th–12th century, Nigeria.

An modern Muslim Yoruba woman.

In addition to those five categories, there is a vital force, a power or energy permeating the whole universe. For the Yoruba, every plant, animal and natural phenomenon is a carrier of the divine. God is the source and the ultimate controller of the vital forces and the deities are the intermediaries between man and god.

A few human beings are endowed with the knowledge and ability to tap, manipulate and use the vital forces: these include medicine men, witches, priests and rainmakers. Some use this knowledge for good; others use it to cause harm to their communities and fellow human beings. In order to appease the gods, people must perform rituals and make sacrifices. There are numerous rituals such as those for the fertility of humans, crops and animals; for birth, initiation, marriage and death; and for rainmaking, planting and harvesting.

Yggdrasil: the world tree
Scandinavia

In Norse mythology, Yggdrasil is a giant ash tree that holds nine worlds in its roots, trunk and branches. Those nine worlds are:

> **Midgard** (world of humanity)
> **Asgard** (world of the Aesir)
> **Vanaheim** (world of the Vanir – the other tribe of gods)
> **Jotunheim** (world of the giants)
> **Niflheim** (primordial world of ice)
> **Muspelheim** (primordial world of fire)
> **Alfheim** (world of the elves)
> **Svartalheim** (world of the dwarves)
> **Hel** (world of the dead)

Three Norns guard Yggdrasil. Those Norns are the three women who decide the fate and fortune of each human. They visit each newborn baby and choose the life the child will lead. An eagle watches over the top of the tree with all of the secrets of the universe.

Midgard sits between the worlds of the gods and the underworld, occupied by humans. A sea inhabited by the Midgard serpent surrounds this world.

This world tree, Yggdrasil, is watered by the Well of Urd ('destiny'). The water is said to be so holy it turns anything it has been in contact with white. This myth is understood not to have a physical location. Rather, it is a concept that lives inside everything.

Frozen fjord and mountain peaks in Norway.

The Ash Yggdrasil. *The world tree Yggdrasil and some of its inhabitants by Friedrich Wilhelm Heine (1845–1921).*

World Tree

An *axis mundi* (also known as a cosmic axis, world pillar or world tree) is in some mythologies the connection between heaven and earth at the centre of the world.

The sky ladder
World mythologies

In ancient times, the sky and earth were thought accessible and connected by ladders. This was a regular feature of many world mythologies.

Deities and immortals can go up and down those ladders whenever they choose, and some humans with magic powers also have access. There are two types of sky ladders: those made from trees and those made from mountains.

In ancient Chinese mythology, a place called Duguang – thought to be modern-day Chengdu – is the centre of heaven and earth. A special kind of tree, called a Lingshou, grows there and it is those trees that lead to heaven. As they grow in the centre of heaven and earth, the sun shines directly above the trees and they leave no shadow.

In West African folklore, communication between the gods/spirits in the sky and the men is via a sky ladder. The sky ladder is also a common motif in Australian Aboriginal mythology.

There is also the story of Jacob's Ladder in the Bible: a ladder that connects earth and heaven. However, this ladder appears in a dream and therefore is of symbolic reference.

The ladder has often come to represent not only the connection between heaven and earth, but also the history of mankind, with each rung of the ladder representing a kingdom that has ruled the world.

Sunshine in the park of Chengdu, thought to be the centre of heaven and earth in Chinese mythology.

Jacob's Ladder, c.1490.

Sun and moon
World mythologies

The sun, as source of warmth and light and the marker of time, has great significance in many world mythologies. As the sun appears to move each day, people have assumed it is being controlled by an external force. For example, in Egyptian mythology, the sun sails in a barge, and in Greek mythology, it is transported by chariot.

The face of Tonatiuh, from the central disk of an Aztec calendar.

Sun worship is central to many south and central American people. An Aztec sun god, Huitzilopochtli, is fed with human sacrifices. The Aztecs had five sun gods, and believed that the sun dies at the end of each cosmic era. The fifth and final sun god being Tonatiuh, who is believed to be the sun we have today.

The moon is seen as a symbol for many things, including love, desire, change, fertility and passion.

The Native American Algonquian tribe have different names for the full moon in each month, related to nature and the seasons, such as Wolf Moon in January, when hungry wolves howl at night, and Pink Moon in April, on account of a type of pink flower that begins to bloom in this month.

The Inuit, the indigenous people of Alaska, Greenland and the Arctic, explain the existence of the sun and the moon with the legend of the moon god Anningan and his sister, the sun goddess Malina. The two live together until one day they quarrel. Malina leaves and Anningan follows her. The pursuit continues for a long time and Anningan forgets to eat and becomes extremely thin. This accounts for the waning phase of the moon. When the moon vanishes completely it is understood that Anningan is looking for food. These cycles of pursuit, pause and finally catching his sister account for the waxing and waning of the moon and the solar eclipse.

Hieroglyphic art of the sun god Ra.

Moon rabbit

Ra (or Re) is the ancient Egyptian sun god and creator of the world, usually portrayed with a hawk's head and sitting on a fiery orange disc like the sun.

The sun is typically depicted as male, and the moon as female. In Chinese mythology, Chang'e is a woman who lives on the moon. She was once an immortal who becomes mortal as a result of her bad behaviour; trying to regain her immortality, she takes a magic pill, but then gets greedy, takes too many and floats up to the moon. She is eventually allowed to have a companion on the moon. This is the moon rabbit (also called the jade rabbit).

The moon goddess is called Selene in Greek mythology and Luna in Roman mythology. In both cases she is paired with the god of the sun; he travels during the day and she takes over at night.

According to the Shinto religion in Japan, Tsuki-Yomi is the moon god who lives in the heavens with his sister, the sun goddess Amaterasu. Tsuki-Yomi was born from the right eye of the primeval man Izanagi.

Tribal gods
Scandinavia

In Norse mythology, gods and goddesses usually belong to one of two tribes: the Aesir or the Vanir. In most of the tales, the tribes cooperate with each other most of the time. Freya, the Vanir goddess, practises magic and goes from town to town plying her craft for hire. She arrives in the home of the Aesir, who are impressed by her powers. They all seek her services, but then quickly realize that their values and morals are being compromised in their selfish desire to benefit from her magic. Three times they attempt to murder Freya by setting fire to her, but each time she rises from the ashes.

Freya (or Frigg), goddess of love in Scandinavian mythology. Freya is the wife of the god Odin.

'At this signal the other Aesir threw the chain round the monster's neck.' An illustration from Heroes of Asgard, Tales from Scandinavian Mythology, *by A. and E. Keary.*

This leads to war between the Aesir and the Vanir, which continues for a long period. Eventually, the two tribes of divinities call a truce and pay tribute to each other by sending two hostages to live with the opposition. Vanir's Freya and Njord go to the Aesir. Aesir's Mimir and Hoenir go to the Vanir, but Hoenir is a simpleton and is not very helpful, and is responsible for his friend Mimir's death by beheading. Although this doesn't start another war, Odin is distraught and embalms Mimir's head.

Stealing the sun
Congo

Several cultures have myths about the theft of the sun.

According to central African mythology, Mokele is the sun god, a young and handsome man who lives near Lake Tumba (or Lake Ntomba), in what is now the Democratic Republic of Congo. He is the culture hero of the Ntomba tribe, who live around Lake Ntomba. Mokele is a healer and has a supernatural powder called kangili-kangili that he sprinkles on the dead to bring them back to life. He is considered ancestor to a long line of heroes and warriors who appear in the tribal myths.

Mokele is the son of the tribal chief and his favourite wife. His father, the first male human, has been eagerly anticipating the birth of his first child for some time. Mokele's conception was unusual: undertaken by a river goddess who, after implanting the egg in his mother's belly transfers it to her own for its development. When Mokele is born, he instantly begins to age and in this accelerated manner is the size of a four year old

A photograph from 1910 of drummers at Lake Ntomba in the Democratic Republic of the Congo.

on his second day of life. On his fourth day, Mokele's father is still unaware of his son's existence. After returning from hunting, Mokele's father hears the cries of the child from the hut. Mokele gets his father's attention in a most dramatic fashion by using supernatural powers to open the doors of the hut and create a path for his father, unrolling woven mats for him to approach. Mokele then greets his father and explains that he is his son.

Another tribal leader, Chief Mokulaka, has stolen the sun, so while the bright moon shines at night, there are only grey overcast skies during the day. Mokele wants to give the sun back to his people, so he chops down a tree to build a canoe and sail to Chief Mokulaka. Some animals go with him to help including a tortoise, a hawk and wasps. When Mokele arrives Chief Mokulaka asks him to stay for lunch, but he instructs his daughter to put poison in the food. When the daughter sees that Mokele is so handsome she pours the poison away. In the meantime, the tortoise finds the sun's hiding place and gives it to the hawk to return to the sky. The hawk lifts the sun high into the sky, so that its light illuminates the earth. Mokele, the chief's daughter, and all the animals hop into his canoe just as Chief Mokulaka's eldest son returns home with his warriors. They chase Mokele's boat, but the wasps sting the warriors so fiercely that they soon turn back. Every day since then, the hawk has hauled the sun into the sky from east to west, following the route of the flowing waters of Lake Tumba and Congo rivers.

An African sunset as the hawk carries the sun from east to west.

Stealing the sun

The origins of the seasons
North America

Each of the hundreds of tribes across the landmass of North America retains a vivid distinctiveness in their stories and myths. However, each tribe's mythological tool-box also reveals commonalities which unify all these many and varied peoples across the country.

As with all indigenous people across the globe, now self-described as First Nation peoples, in Native American culture the land and the natural world carry the central organizing principles for every aspect of life: practical, spiritual and philosophical. There is perfect harmony in the natural world and humans are a part of this ecosystem. All entities, in creation are reliant upon each other, but each also possesses its own unique spirit – a belief known as *animism*. There are always solutions to resolve conflict, and disruptions only come from the interference of outside forces.

In a culture of storytellers with an oral tradition, these myths were circulated over millennia, mouth to ear, and remain embedded in the bone and sinew of the people, whether they still have access to lands or have been dispossessed.

The ingenious way tribes explained the baffling reality of the changing of seasons is a breathtaking act of imagination. These cultures sought explanations for profound everyday phenomena such as the world moving through dark and light, temperature fluctuations from cold to scorching, abundance and scarcity of food and livestock, when birds leave *en masse* for warmer climes, and why trees lose their leaves.

The idea of 'earth-diving' describes how the world, originally filled with water, becomes solid when animals who are able to dive to the ocean floor bring back soil to the surface. After the world has been populated, there is discord due to a lack of contrast when it is always warm and pleasant. From here a contest begins between sundry characters on desired alternatives: the trickster Coyote proposes an unwieldy forty seasons.

A Lakota chief, known as Red Hawk, dressed in traditional clothing of the Oglala people, photographed in 1905.

Sunshine over the Grand Teton mountain range of the Rocky Mountains. The spiritual aspects of weather, seasons and light remain hugely important throughout most North American mythologies.

Wonder Lake in McKinley, Denali National Park, Alaska. The belief that every part of the ecosystem, including animals, trees and bodies of water, possesses its own unique spirit is a common theme throughout the First Nation peoples of North America.

THE GREAT SPIRIT

Into this setting of general discord with a changeless state of existence steps the 'Great Spirit', or 'Old Man'. Nobody notices him arrive and he asks households for support with food and shelter and is rejected by people unwilling to part with their possessions. Finally, he comes upon the household least able to help and they are happy to share with him. His edict, delivered from the sky the following day, is a punishment: the invention of seasons. Hardship follows abundance and resources must be rationed. It's a moral message, an end to the paradise of stability.

Plains, Forest, and Polar are the categories of this land where weather always has spiritual aspects. There are poetic flourishes within this cosmology and, always, humour that is sharp. Seasons are personified, and conflict and its resolution used to teach lessons in how to live in extreme weather.

Time

The time line in mythic tales is often hard to follow. Ancient storytellers did not feel the need to follow the linear experience of time as we live with it. Children may become older than their parents, for example, and entire periods may be written off in the storytelling arc so that an important future deity spends 700 years gestating in his mother's womb and is born as a wizened old man. Therefore a suspension of disbelief is required in order to enable the reader to grasp the most important elements of the myth.

The eternal cycle
India

In Indian mythology, time is inconsequential. It is the most fluid system we have information about. There is a continuum within everything. Past, present and future all have equal importance and, indeed, are regarded as the same. Everything is cyclical so there are no surprises. Every action has happened before. Every entity has existed before and the current deities are merely the latest versions in a timeless cycle. The universe has been made and destroyed infinite times, and our current universe is but one version of many. This idea of the fluidity of time allowed storytellers of old to give free rein to their imagination, operating within established themes of replenishment and order.

Pilgrims bath in the river Ganges in Varanasi, India, to celebrate Maha Shivaratri, an ancient festival honouring the god Shiva. According to Indian mythology, Shiva is responsible for creation, preservation and destruction throughout the universe.

Mayan calendar
Mesoamerica

The Maya are recognized as being among the greatest astronomer-mathematicians of any civilization. They developed a system that allowed them to make predictions about events on a local, global and cosmic scale.

For example, the Maya predicted that the end of the world would occur on 21 December 2012. It was Mayan belief that this date marked the end of a cycle, after which another cycle would immediately begin.

Each cycle (pik or bak'tun – both words mean 'cycle') was a period of 144,000 days (about 394 years) in the ancient Mayan Long Count system. In this system, time is measured from a mythical beginning of the current age until a distant point in the future when it is believed that the age will come to a close. In this case 21 December 2012 marks the end of the thirteenth pik, and is also regarded as the end of a significant cycle, made up of thirteen cycles (5122 years).

The Chichén Itzá temple, built by the Mayan people.

The Dreaming
Australia

One of the features of the cosmology of the Aboriginal peoples of Australia is the interconnectedness of everything in the life cycle. Customary laws, handed down and enacted in ceremonies spanning almost 60,000 years, embody traditional belief about the physical creation of the land and the animals in it. Their mythology describes their connection with animals, birds and the creatures of the sea. Other stories explain the sun, for instance, through the figure of a woman who carries a piece of blazing bark in her mountain climb each morning. Along the route her red ochre body paint colours the clouds and at the far western horizon she puts out her bark torch before returning to the underground. Then begins her next daily ritual going back to the east to collect her blazing bark in order to bring a bright start to the next new day.

This Dhautaupil bark painting from Arnhem Land, Northern Territory, features Dreamtime figures.

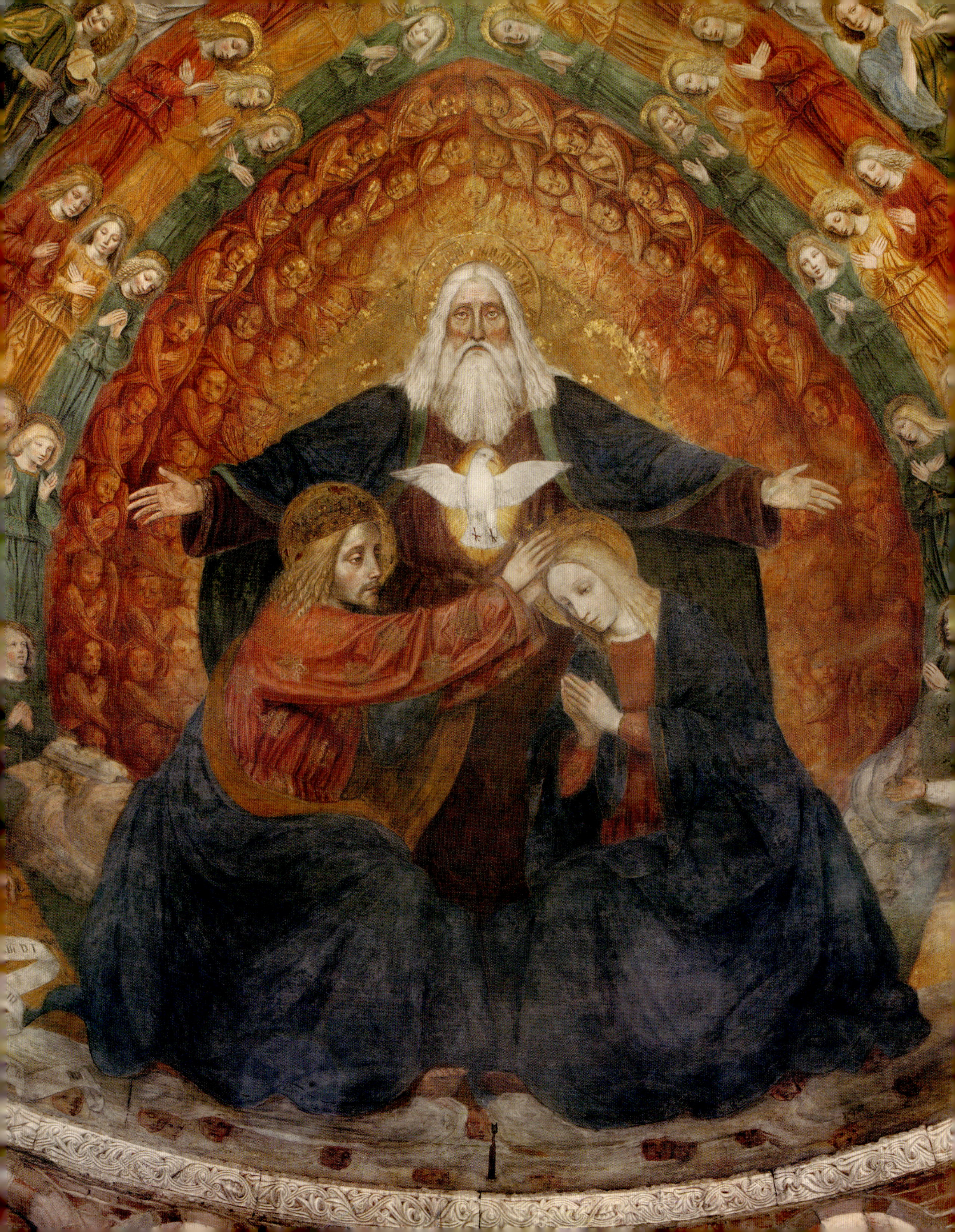

Stories of gods and men

One version of the Greek creation myth sees men and women as springing up naturally from Gaia (Mother Earth). They were created in the same way as all other animals and plants. There have been Five Ages of mortals. In the Golden Age, Cronus (also Saturn) rules the universe, and it is serene. In the Silver Age mortals are happy, but lack ideas and have become generally useless. Zeus, leader of the gods, ends that age in a huge flood.

In the first Bronze Age, the new batch of human beings are only interested in war, and effectively destroy themselves. In the second Bronze Age, the surviving mortals mate with the gods and produce heroes such as Achilles and Heracles. War is still popular and humans still flawed but there are now opportunities to flourish and improve. Most Greek heroic myth-stories date from this age.

The Age of Iron, our present age, finds humans still as destructive as before but now abandoned by the gods. It may be that the time will soon come when humans are swept away so that the world can start afresh with the sixth age, a New Golden Age.

POSEIDON
GREECE

Poseidon is one of the twelve main deities of ancient Greek mythology. These gods are known as the Olympians as they live on Mount Olympus. Immortal and unchanging, the Olympians father a huge array of demigods, spirits, other deities and humans as a result of their numerous unions with gods and mortals.

The Triumph of Neptune, a mosaic found in the House of Wadi Blibane, Sousse, in Tunisia.

Poseidon (who is known as Neptune in Roman mythology) is the child of Cronus and Rhea and elder brother of Zeus. It is told that Cronus fears that his children will ultimately destroy him and so he aims to swallow them all, including Poseidon and Zeus. In some traditions, Rhea hides Poseidon and replaces him with a foal that Chronus devours instead.

Poseidon is ruler of the sea. He controls the waves with his trident, a three-pronged spear, and can provoke floods, storms and earthquakes.

STORIES OF GODS AND MEN

He has a magnificent palace, glittering with gold, under the Aegean Sea. His reputation is as a violent, vindictive and dangerous god.

He is usually depicted holding his trident as he rides a chariot pulled by monstrous half-horse, half-serpent creatures, surrounded by fish and dolphins. Besides being the god of the sea, Poseidon is credited with giving the first horse to man.

Poseidon's legitimate wife is the goddess Amphitrite, with whom he has no children. But he has six sons and a daughter named Rhodes with his lover, the sea nymph Halia. The island where Rhodes was born is named after her. Poseidon went on to father many more children through his numerous love affairs. Those children are generally violent and evil.

Theseus is the son of Poseidon, straddling the divide between divine and mortal. On the night she conceives, Theseus's mother sleeps with both Poseidon and Aegeus, King of Athens.

Poseidon helps mortals to build the walls of Troy, but when King Laomedon refuses to pay Poseidon an agreed salary for his help, the god of the sea summons a sea monster to attack the Trojans. This marks the beginning of Poseidon's resentment against the Trojans; in the Trojan War, he fights on the side of the Greeks.

Statue of Poseidon, one of the twelve main deities of Greek mythology.

ACHILLES
GREECE

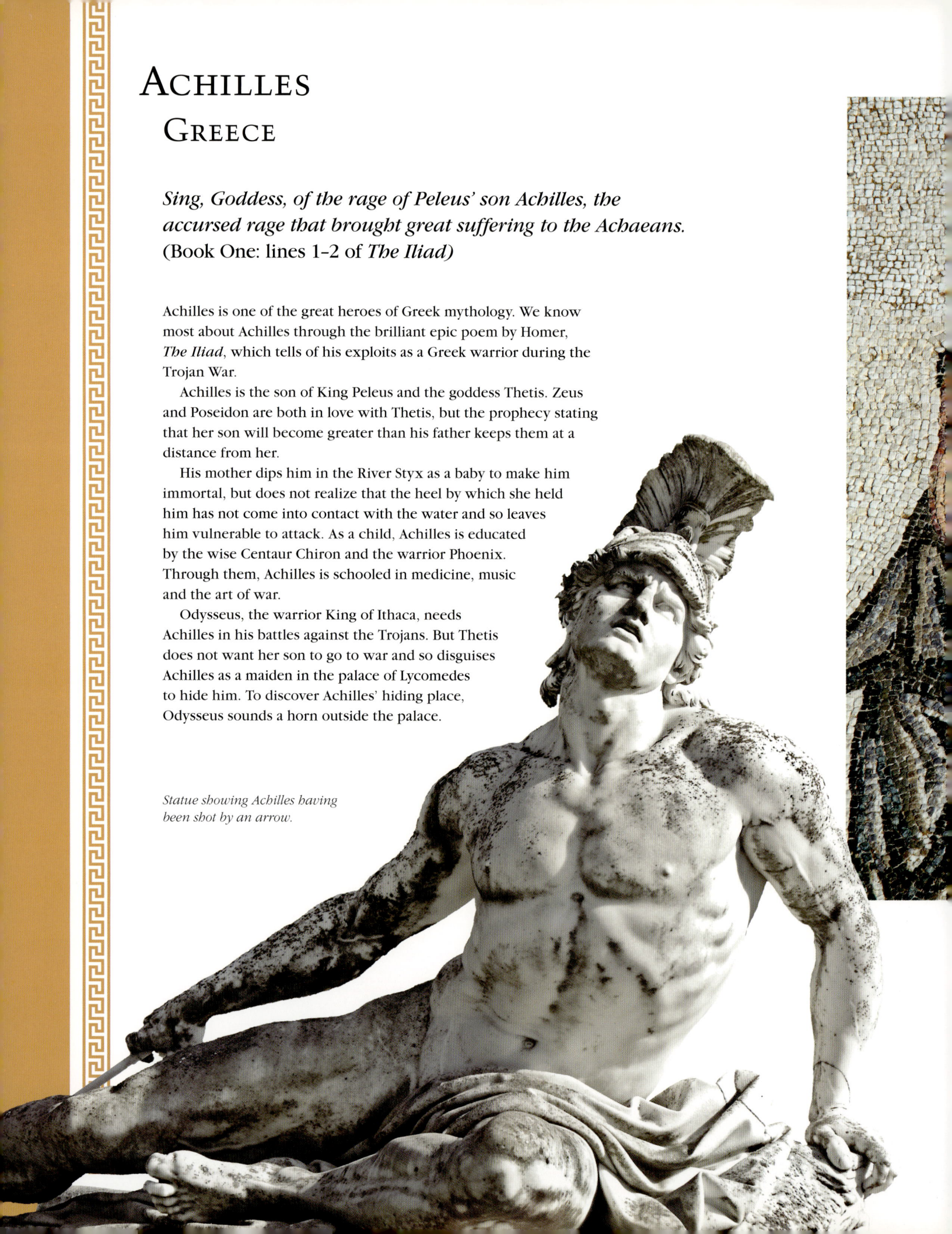

Sing, Goddess, of the rage of Peleus' son Achilles, the accursed rage that brought great suffering to the Achaeans.
(Book One: lines 1–2 of *The Iliad*)

Achilles is one of the great heroes of Greek mythology. We know most about Achilles through the brilliant epic poem by Homer, *The Iliad*, which tells of his exploits as a Greek warrior during the Trojan War.

Achilles is the son of King Peleus and the goddess Thetis. Zeus and Poseidon are both in love with Thetis, but the prophecy stating that her son will become greater than his father keeps them at a distance from her.

His mother dips him in the River Styx as a baby to make him immortal, but does not realize that the heel by which she held him has not come into contact with the water and so leaves him vulnerable to attack. As a child, Achilles is educated by the wise Centaur Chiron and the warrior Phoenix. Through them, Achilles is schooled in medicine, music and the art of war.

Odysseus, the warrior King of Ithaca, needs Achilles in his battles against the Trojans. But Thetis does not want her son to go to war and so disguises Achilles as a maiden in the palace of Lycomedes to hide him. To discover Achilles' hiding place, Odysseus sounds a horn outside the palace.

Statue showing Achilles having been shot by an arrow.

Achilles thinks the palace is being attacked and rushes for his weapons, giving himself away in the process. So Achilles cannot escape his destiny. He goes to war at the age of fifteen leading fifty ships, seeking fame and glory, despite a prophecy that says he will not come back alive. In this conflict, Achilles is the commander of the Myrmidons, the legendary people of Thessaly created by Zeus from a colony of ants.

The most notable feat of the Trojan War is the killing of the Trojan hero Hector outside the gates of Troy. Achilles is a key player in this war. He is a ruthless fighter but an arrow shot into his heel, the only vulnerable part of his body, finally kills him. The phrase 'Achilles' heel' continues to be used to denote a point of weakness.

Achilles as a child, from the 4th-century Roman mosaic of the first bath of Achilles at the Villa of Theseus, Paphos Archaeological Park, Cyprus.

Achilles 83

Zeus and his thunderbolts
Greece

Zeus is the god of light, the skies and thunder and is generally regarded as the greatest god of the Greek pantheon. He is King of men and gods, enthroned in the sky and linked to the symbol of the eagle. He maintains order and justice in the world.

Zeus – king of the gods, the ruler of Mount Olympus and the god of the sky and thunder.

He is also the distributor of good and evil, which are kept in two jars at the entrance to his palace. It is Zeus who decides on the proportion of good and evil each mortal will comprise, thus deciding their destiny.

Zeus is the last-born son of Cronus and Rhea. Cronus has been warned that one of his sons will dethrone him and so he plans to devour his children as Rhea gives birth to them. When Zeus is due to be born, Rhea goes into a cave in Crete and gives birth in the night, hides the child and gives Cronus a stone wrapped in a blanket to eat instead. Zeus is saved and goes into hiding.

When Zeus reaches adulthood, he gives Cronus a drug that makes him vomit up the children he has swallowed. His brothers and sisters, restored to life, help Zeus defeat Cronus and the Titans. Zeus is given the sky, thunder and lightning; his brother Poseidon is given a trident to control the sea, and Hades is granted invisibility and power over the Underworld.

Zeus' next battle is against the Giants, whom he defeats. The giant Enceladus is buried under the island of Sicily and, even today, when the giant turns over, the whole island shakes.

His final battle is against the monster Typhoeus. Zeus is injured and captured by the monster but is then rescued by Hermes. Zeus resumes the struggle and finally overwhelms the monster with his thunderbolts. This triple victory ensures that no gods or mortals will ever attempt to fight Zeus again, and he retains his rank of uncontested master.

Zeus's infidelities are legendary and he fathers many children, including some with his own sisters. His children include Athena, Aphrodite and Apollo.

An engraving by Michelangelo shows Zeus sending to earth with a thunderbolt Phaeton and his out-of-control chariot with four horses, which resulted in the burning of Mount Oeta and the drying of the Libyan desert.

Zeus and his thunderbolts

THE TROJAN WAR
GREECE

The Greeks consider the Trojan War, which supposedly occured between the 11th and 12th centuries BC, as both the end of the mythical age and the beginning of the historical age. Modern archeological findings at the alleged location of the citadel suggest that the fall of Troy may have more historical roots than previously thought.

According to the *Iliad* (also see pages 174–5), the goddesses Hera, Athena and Aphrodite are arguing over who is the most beautiful of the three. They visit Paris, prince of Troy, and ask him to choose between them. Paris chooses Aphrodite. In return, she promises him the most beautiful mortal woman for his wife. Unfortunately, Helen, the most beautiful woman in the world, is already married to Menelaus, the king of Sparta. Paris, son of the Trojan King Priam, kidnaps Helen and returns with her to the city of Troy. Menelaus is furious and convinces the rest of Greece to go to war against the Trojans. The Greeks fight the Trojans for years, but the city has tall, strong walls that make it impregnable.

The *Iliad* begins nine years into the Trojan War, starting with a quarrel between Achilles and Agamemnon over a female slave. Following that dispute, Achilles withdraws from the war. The Trojans, led by Hector, almost defeat the Greeks. When Hector kills Achilles' close friend, Patroclus, Achilles rejoins the war and kills Hector.

The Trojan War is brought to a close when the Greeks use subterfuge to enter Troy. They behave as though they have accepted defeat, dismantle their camps and march away, as if going for good, leaving a huge wooden horse behind as a peace offering. The Trojans accept the gift and drag it into the city. Unknown to them, Greek soldiers are hidden inside the horse. At night, while the Trojans are feasting, soldiers climb out of the wooden horse and open the gates, allowing the rest of the Greek army to enter and capture the city.

Importantly, the story of the Trojan horse does not appear in the *Iliad*. Instead, this story comes from Virgil's *Aeneid* written much later during the time of Emperor Augustus. The *Aeneid* tells the story of Aeneas, a Trojan hero and son of Prince Anchises and the goddess Aphrodite (Venus), who survives the war. He escapes with a number of other survivors who set off to find a new homeland. After first traveling to Carthage, they eventually arrive on the banks of the river Tiber. The *Aeneid* conveniently conflates two much older mythologies: the legend of Troy from the Late Helladic period and the indigenous Roman story of the twins Romulas and Remus (see also pages 214-5). According to Virgil's account, Aeneas is an ancestor of Romulus and Remus.

The Siege of Troy *by Biagio di Antonio (1476–1504)*.

A scene from the Iliad *by Michael Martin Drolling (1786–1851)*.

The Trojan War

Marrying mortals
Greece

Mortal-born heroes and heroines can be elevated to divine status through marriage to a god, but tales of such unions rarely have happy endings.

Ariadne is the daughter of King Minos of Crete. She falls in love with Theseus when he comes to Crete to battle the Minotaur. She flees with Theseus, but he abandons her on the island of Naxos. Dionysus, the god of wine, mystic ecstasy and orgiastic excess, discovers her there and makes her his wife. Dionysus takes her into Heaven and she

A 19th-century depiction of Ariadne by Asher Brown Durand.

STORIES OF GODS AND MEN

is his consort in his pleasures and performances across the universe. It is either Dionysus or Aphrodite, goddess of love, who gives her a crown of seven stars. On her death, the crown is positioned in the sky as her everlasting memorial and is named the Corona Borealis.

Tithonus is a Trojan prince, son of King Laomedon of Troy. He is very handsome, and so Eos, goddess of the Dawn, kidnaps him, and takes him to Ethiopia to be her lover. She asks Zeus to grant Tithonus immortality, which he does, but she forgets to ask also for his eternal youth. Tithonus becomes older and older, and shrinks as he does so. He becomes so small that Eos puts him in a wicker basket like a baby, and eventually turns him into a cicada.

Psyche is such a lovely young girl that men are daunted by her beauty and she remains unwed. Psyche's sisters all find husbands and so her father is keen that she should also marry and consults an oracle for advice. The oracle says that Psyche must be dressed for marriage and left on a rock, where a monster will come and take possession of her. Her father obeys the oracle and Psyche is taken from the rock. When she wakes up, she is in the garden of a beautiful palace and has servants to look after her. At night she is aware of a presence lying next to her, and a voice says that this is her husband, but that if she ever sees him she will lose him forever. Psyche is very happy, but she misses her family, so she persuades her husband to allow her to return home for a visit. When her sisters see how happy she is, they are jealous and try to sow doubt in her mind. They advise her to take a lamp back with her and discover what her husband looks like when he is sleeping. On returning, she holds the lamp above her sleeping husband and sees a handsome young figure: the god of love, Eros. When she spills lamp oil on him, he awakes and flees. No longer protected by Eros, Psyche wanders the earth being pursued by Aphrodite, who is jealous of her beauty. Eventually, Psyche and Eros are reunited.

There are countless sexual encounters between gods and mortals. The coupling of Zeus with a mortal woman named Leto produces two important gods, Artemis and Apollo.

A terracotta statuette of Eros and Psyche from the 4th century BC.

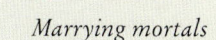

Pele's revenge
Hawaii

Pele, the fire goddess in Hawaiian mythology, is also goddess of lightning, dance, wind, volcanoes and violence. She is also referred to as Madame Pele or Tutu Pele as a mark of respect. Pele is both creator and destroyer and known for her passion, jealousy and violent temper. She created the islands of Hawaii using her power over the volcanoes and lives in an active volcano at the summit of Kilauea Volcano in the Halemaumau crater. Pele is daughter of Haumea, the earth goddess, and Kane, the creator of the sky.

A statue of Pele, the Hawaiian fire goddess.

After Pele turned Ohi'a into a tree, the gods took pity on Lehua and, so she could always remain close to her lover, they transformed her into the beautiful red flower which you see adorning the twisted branches.

Goddess of lava

There are several geological terms related to volcanoes that are named after the goddess Pele. 'Pele's Hair' is a form of molten lava, and 'Pele's Tears' is a form of solidified lava.

The story of Pele's Revenge tells how a young couple, Ohi'a and Lehua, are very much in love and living happily together. One day, Pele, in human form, is walking in the forest when she sees the handsome young Ohi'a working in his garden. She falls in love with him and wants him for herself but Ohi'a rejects her. When Ohi'a's beautiful young wife Lehua comes into the garden, carrying her husband's midday meal, Pele flies into a jealous rage. She abandons her human disguise and transforms into a raging fire. She turns Ohi'a into an ugly twisted tree in revenge for spurning her advances. Lehua begs Pele to turn her husband back into a man or turn her into a tree as well, but she is ignored. When the other gods see what Pele has done to the innocent young couple, they turn Lehua into a beautiful red flower and plant it at the bottom of Ohi'a's tree. To this day, the Ohia tree in Hawaii blossoms with beautiful red flowers.

The maid of the mist
North America

This is a myth from the Niagara Falls area of North America and is the oldest known legend associated with the waterfall, which has been flowing for more than 12,000 years.

It is told by the Seneca, a group of Native American Iroquoian-speaking people who live near Lake Ontario in north-eastern North America. A young Seneca girl named Lelawala is immortalized in the story as the first and true 'maid of the mist'. Lelawala loses her husband. Wracked with grief at her bereavement, she decides to take her canoe and row over the Falls. She prays to the storm god Heno to make her death quick, but he decides to rescue her instead. He catches her in his arms and takes her to live with him and his family beneath the water. The grieving girl

Niagara Falls, where legend has it that the echo of Heno's voice can still be heard.

A Seneca woman, Ah-Weh-Eyu (Pretty Flower), photographed in 1908. Lelawala belonged to the Seneca peoples of this region and her legendary story is inextricably tied with the features of this dramatic natural landscape.

is well looked after and soon recovers. Heno's youngest son falls in love with her and they marry and have a son. Lelawala is happy, but misses her people.

One day, a giant snake comes down to the river and poisons the water of her people. Heno gives her the news, and she begs him to allow her home for one hour. She travels home and warns her people to flee and move to higher ground. When the snake comes back to feast on the bodies of the people it has poisoned, it finds an empty village. In the serpent's rage, it destroys Heno's underwater home, but Heno manages to kill it with a thunderbolt. Heno takes Lelawala, along with his sons and his grandson, through the water of the Falls and into the clouds, where they build a new home. There is a legend that you can hear the echo of Heno's voice in the thunder of the water of Niagara Falls.

The maid of the mist

War with the Titans
Greece

In Greek mythology, the Titans most famously include the first pantheon of Greek gods. They are the six sons and six daughters of Uranus and Gaea: Kronos, Iapetus, Hyperion, Oceanus, Coeus, Creus, Theia, Rhea, Mnemosyne, Phoebe, Tethys, and Themis. The later generation, led by Zeus, are known as the Olympian gods. They are made up of the gods Zeus, Poseidon, Apollo, Hermes, Ares and Hephaestus, and the goddesses Athene, Artemis, Hera, Aphrodite, Hestia and Demeter.

Battle of the Titans, attributed to Francesco Allegrini, c.1615.

The Titans, led by Kronos, depose their father and rule the universe. Based on Mount Othrys are jealous of the new gods of Mount Olympus and launch an attack on the Olympians that lasts ten years. This battle between the gods causes chaos and disruption, with earthquakes, fires and lightning.

The Olympians, led by Zeus, have formidable weapons. They include Hades' helmet of darkness, Poseidon's trident, and Zeus' thunderbolts. They are also aided by the three Hecatoncheires, 100-handed monsters named Briareus, Gyges, and Cottus.

Kronos, *by 17th-century artist Giacinto Brandi. Kronos was one of the Greek Titans and father of Zeus. He was known as Saturn in Roman mythology.*

With these weapons, Zeus and his brothers are finally able to defeat the Titans after a bitter war and the new pantheon is established at Mount Olympus. After the struggle, Zeus punishes the vanquished Titans, including condemning Iapetus' son, Atlas, to carry the sky on his shoulders.

After this victory, Zeus and the Olympians become immortal and unchanging. Zeus is ruler of the sky, Poseidon of the seas and Hades of the underworld. A new era of Greek mythology has commenced.

Devas against Asuras
India

In classical Hindu mythology, Devas are divine beings and Asuras are demons. Both are gifted with remarkable and mysterious powers – Devas use their powers for good and Asuras for evil.

Deva is the masculine word for 'heavenly, divine, anything of excellence'; the feminine equivalent is Devi. The Hindu goddess Devi represents the 'divine feminine'.

Devas have qualities such as generosity, forgiveness, truthfulness, austerity, cleanliness and self-control, whereas Asuras have demonic qualities like arrogance, cheating and ignorance. Devas and Asuras are often portrayed in the mythology as being at war with one another.

Surya (the sun) is called the 'Asura-chaplain of the Devas'. Devas and Asuras both come from the same ancestor, Prajapati, but the Devas choose truth over falsehood, and the Asuras choose the opposite.

This picture shows the goddess Durga, who is an incarnation of the anger of Vishnu and Shiva, vanquishing the buffalo demon Mahishasura in one of the great battles between the Devas and the Asuras. It originates from Bikaner, Rajasthan, and dates from c.1275.

At first their lies make the Asuras strong, but eventually they lead to destruction; the Devas begin weak but attain prosperity and power by telling the truth.

The Devas sometimes assume different and terrible shapes to fight the Asuras. For example, Vishnu may take the form of a cruel monster with a lion's head when he devours his victims.

Shiva's wife Parvati is shown as a beautiful young woman, but she transforms into as many as ten different terrifying creatures in order to defeat the demons.

The Asuras are not always easy to defeat and so the Devas are not always victorious; Asuras have great powers and are sometimes superior to the Devas.

Jalandhara is king of the Asuras. He possesses remarkable powers that threaten to overpower the Devas. Jalandhara's wife is the beautiful Vrinda – a humble woman who is a devotee of Vishnu and Shiva. Jalandhara hears about the goddess Parvati's beauty and so, disguised as Shiva, he goes to her. Parvati recognizes the deception and summons the power of the real Shiva. He is furious and goes into battle to kill the demon Jalandhara. However, Jalandhara survives because of his extraordinary powers, which are strengthened by his wife Vrinda's loyalty.

Vrinda has received blessings from the gods that her husband can never die as long as she remains true to him. Lord Vishnu, who also has the power to shape-shift, decides to pay Jalandhara back for his trickery. Vishnu goes to Vrinda's house disguised as Jalandhara. Unlike Parvati, Vrinda does not recognize the deception. Her fidelity to her husband is broken and as a result Jalandhara loses his power and is defeated.

A sculpture of Lord Shiva meditating in the lotus position on the Ganges river in Rishikesh. Shiva destroys Jalandhara by deceiving his wife, Vrinda.

Celtic gods against the Fomorians
Ireland

The mythology of the Celts predates Christianity and has been preserved in written form since the Middle Ages. However, the Christian influence during the time of writing means that the spiritual dimensions of these early myths may have been skewed.

The Fomorians are a race of demonic giants who have preceded the gods. They are mythical, prehistoric beings who have raided Ireland from the sea. The Irish word 'Fomoraig' means dark of the sea. According to the legend, they originally came from Asia or Northern Africa, and are usually depicted as having black skin, black hair and a goat-like face.

The Fomorians defeat the Partholons, who are ruling Ireland at this time, by afflicting them with the plague. Another race, the Nemedians, then try to defeat the Fomorians but without success. The Firbolgs are the next to try, and eventually they manage to live peacefully alongside the Fomorians. The king of the Fomorians is Balor, and other notable members included Bres, Tethra and Eriu. Balor is a giant with one large eye in his forehead; when he opens his eye, he wreaks havoc and destruction.

After a period of peace, the Tuatha Dé Danann arrive, travelling on their magic cloud. The Tuatha Dé Danann defeat the Firbolgs at the first battle of Mag Tuireadh. At the

An illustration from Celtic Myth and Legend *by Charles Squire, showing Cian finding Balor's daughter.*

second battle of Mag Tuireadh, they beat the Fomorians, too, but then choose to come to a peaceful agreement with them. The Tuatha Dé Danann give the Fomorians the province of Connacht and even allow them to marry some of the Tuatha Dé Danann and have children by them.

There is a prophecy that Balor will be killed by his own grandson, so he locks his daughter Ethniu inside a tower and well away from all men. Cian of the Dé Danann breaks into the tower and seduces her, and she later gives birth to triplets. Two of them are thrown into the sea, where they became the first seals, but one son survives. This son is named Lug and goes on to lead the Tuatha Dé Danann in battle against the Fomorians. He fulfils the prophecy by killing his grandfather, Balor.

In Irish mythology, the Fomorians represent the harmful and destructive powers of nature, such as darkness, death and drought. Tuatha Dé Danann, on the other hand, represent growth and civilization.

Ancient Celtic stones.

Celtic gods against the Fomorians

Conflict and competition
Greece

The Return of Persephone by Frederic Leighton, 1891.

Hera and Zeus are siblings who eventually marry. Initially, Zeus's attempts at courtship are unsuccessful, so he resorts to trickery by transforming himself into an injured cuckoo. When Hera picks up the bird and holds it to her breast, he resumes his male form and rapes her. She marries him to cover her shame, and enters into a turbulent union. Hera is a jealous goddess and most stories about her revolve around her plans to take revenge on Zeus for his philandering.

Demeter is the Olympian goddess of agriculture, and when Zeus gives their daughter Persephone away to Hades, their brother, god of the underworld, she retaliates by bringing starvation to mankind. She threatens to kill them all unless her daughter is returned. Hearing this, Zeus sends the messenger god Hermes down to the underworld to fetch Persephone. Hades agrees to let her go, but first he slips some pomegranate seeds into her mouth. Having eaten something in the underworld she will not be able to escape.

Her mother Demeter is overjoyed when Persephone returns but is also suspicious and asks her daughter if she has eaten anything in the underworld. Persephone confirms that she has. Demeter and Hades agree on a compromise: Persephone will spend half the year in the underworld, and the other half with her mother. Demeter, as the goddess of agriculture, makes sure that when her daughter is in the underworld, nothing will grow, and this is how the seasons came about.

A sculpture of Hera, wife and sister of Zeus and protector of marriage, family and married women.

STORIES OF GODS AND MEN

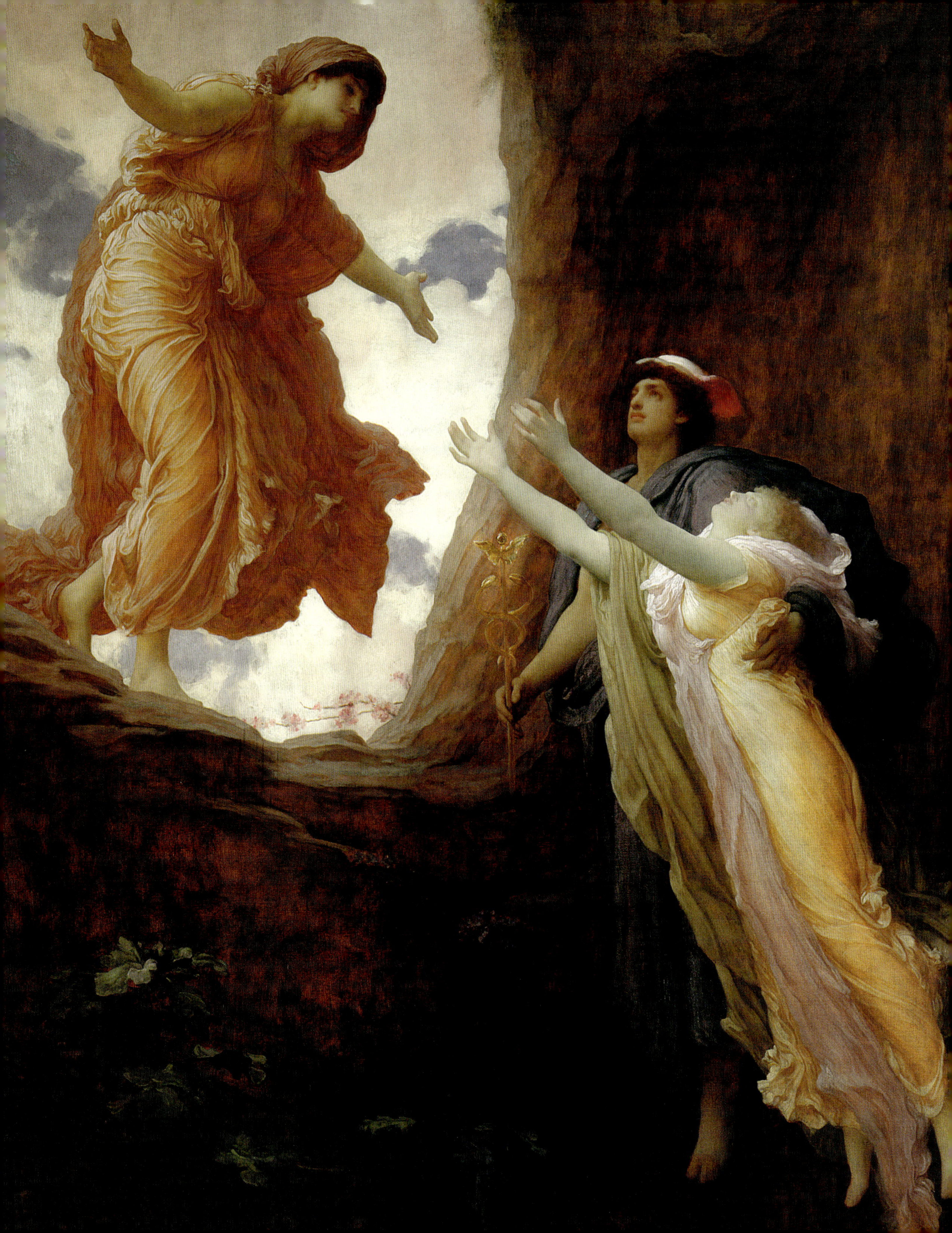

Osiris, Isis and Horus against Set
Egypt

The central triad in ancient Egyptian mythology consists of Osiris, Isis and Horus. There are four children born of Geb, the sky god, and Nut, the earth goddess. The oldest is Osiris, then comes his evil brother Set, and then twin sisters – Isis and Nepthys. Osiris is both a god and the first pharaoh to rule Egypt and, by extension, the world. His queen is his sister, the goddess Isis, who rules Egypt whenever Osiris is travelling. Osiris is a peaceful king who journeys across the earth bringing order and civilization, and teaching mankind about worshipping the gods and how to grow crops.

An ancient Egyptian artwork from the interior wall of a temple in Abydos. The image depicts the falcon-headed god Horus seated on a throne and holding a golden fly whisk. Before him are the Pharaoh Seti and the goddess Isis.

Set is a violent and chaotic god who creates disruption and tries to undo all of Osiris' good work. Despite being kept under surveillance, Set finds the opportunity to attack his brother Osiris and murder him.

Isis is devastated when she discover the body of her husband. She and Osiris do not have children, and with no heirs to the throne Set looks like becoming the next king. Isis is determined to use her magic powers to stop him.

The queen transforms herself into a bird and flies over Osiris' body, using her magic powers to draw Osiris' essence into herself. From this mystic union, Isis conceives and gives birth to Horus. Horus has a falcon's head and eyes that light the world, and as Osiris' son, he is heir to the throne.

An angry Set discovers Osiris's body and cuts it into pieces, scattering the remnants all over Egypt. Isis and her twin sister, Nephthys, journey across the lands to retrieve the body parts. The body is reassembled, treated and wrapped in linen and the twin sisters then stand guard over it.

When Horus grows up, he wants to avenge the death of his father and sets out to battle his uncle Set. In the battle, Set tears out one of Horus's eyes, but Horus ultimately triumphs. The god Thoth later uses his magic to restore Horus's eye. Horus places his healed eye inside his father's body, and Osiris is resurrected. Following the resurrection, the gods hold a trial in which Set is found guilty of murder and condemned to death.

Osiris does not resume the throne; he hands the kingdom of Egypt over to his son Horus, and ascends to heaven where he becomes ruler of the otherworld and judge of the dead. Horus remains the eternal king of Egypt. Every succeeding pharaoh is an incarnation of him.

An amulet from 664–630 BC depicting Nepthys, Horus and Isis.

Osiris, Isis and Horus against Set

Mount Olympus
Greece

Mountains are regarded as the closest points on earth to heaven and so have always been revered as sacred. Mount Olympus is the tallest mountain in Greece, located in the Olympus range in the north of the country, on the border of Macedonia, and approximately 80 km (50 miles) southwest of Thessaloniki. In the time of the gods, no humans were allowed access to the mountain under any circumstances.

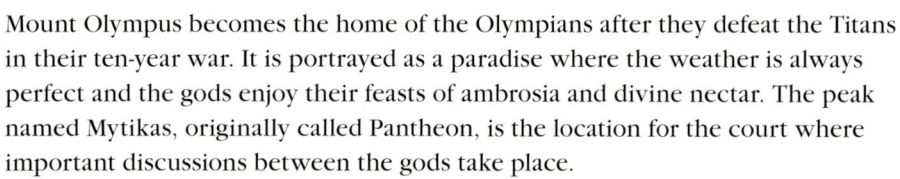

Concourse of the Gods on Mount Olympus, *an engraving by Cornelius Cort, c.1565.*

Mount Olympus becomes the home of the Olympians after they defeat the Titans in their ten-year war. It is portrayed as a paradise where the weather is always perfect and the gods enjoy their feasts of ambrosia and divine nectar. The peak named Mytikas, originally called Pantheon, is the location for the court where important discussions between the gods take place.

Zeus' throne is in a different location, now named Stefani. Every god possesses a private palace on the mountain, but they feast together to discuss the fate of the world and the mortals they rule.

The twelve Olympians reside at Mount Olympus and nine muses live at the foot of the mountain. The nine muses are patrons of the fine arts: Calliope (epic

The southern side of the Greek mountain of gods, Mount Olympus.

poetry), Clio (history), Erato (love poetry), Euterpe (music), Melpomene (tragedy), Polyhymnia (hymns), Terpsichore (dance), Thalia (comedy) and Urania (astronomy).

A mortal named Bellerophon tries to ride the winged horse Pegasus up to Olympus, but is sent a painful reminder that only gods are allowed there. Zeus sends a fly to attack Pegasus, who kicks and rears, throwing Bellerophon from his back; Bellerophon survives but is injured and blinded in the fall.

The Olympians' rule over Mount Olympus is uncontested until the monster gods, under the rule of Typhon, challenge Zeus for control. Together the Olympians are victorious, but the battle is often regarded as the hardest one ever fought in Greek mythology.

Asgard

Scandinavia

In Norse mythology, Asgard is one of the Nine Worlds and the realm and fortress of the Aesir, one of the two tribes of gods. The Nine Worlds are the homelands of various types of beings found in the pre-Christian worldview. They are all held in the branches and roots of the world tree, Yggdrasil.

The Ride of the Valkyries *by John Charles Dollman (1909).*

The Nine Worlds are made up of Asgard, Alfheim, Svartalheim, Midgard, Jotunheim, Vanaheim, Niflheim, Muspelheim and Hel (see page 64).

Asgard is located in the sky and divided into twelve realms, including Valhalla, the home of Odin, and Thrudheim, the home of Thor. Each god has his own palace in Asgard. The gods, under the orders of Odin, have built Asgard themselves. The great wall around Asgard has been built by the frost giant Hrimthurs. The most important gods in Asgard are Odin and Thor. The most perplexing god is Loki, the trickster.

Asgard is an entire and fortified country where the gods own palaces, farms and meadows and spend their days in much the same way as the human landowners in Midgard, tending their crops and animals, hunting, and feasting in their banquet hall Gladsheim, their 'joy-home'. Asgard is connected to Midgard by the rainbow bridge Bifröst.

A woodcut from 1880 showing a Nordic seer discovering Asgard, home of the gods.

The Valkyries, the women who work for Odin, pluck the bravest of the fallen warriors from battlefields in Midgard and take them to Valhalla to eat and drink, and wait for Ragnarok, the end of the universe, where the forces of evil will rise up to do battle with the powers of light. At the end of the myth, Asgard is overwhelmed and its walls and inhabitants pass from existence leaving no trace of their occupation.

TRIPARTITE GOD OF CHRISTIANITY
MIDDLE EAST

The Christian doctrine of the Trinity holds that God is in three parts or hypostases: the Father, the Son (Jesus Christ) and the Holy Spirit. The three are of one essence or nature and make up one true God, equally and eternally. The Trinity, which resides in Heaven, is fundamental to Christianity.

There is frequent use of the pronouns 'our' and 'us' in the Bible rather than 'my' or 'me'. However, the first of the ten commandments is, 'Thou shall have no other gods besides me.' This use of the pronoun 'me', determines that it is one God made up of three parts.

Judaism maintains a tradition of monotheism and excludes the possibility of a Trinity, while Islam states that the doctrine of the Trinity is blasphemous.

Christians believe in the concept of man also as a trinity, made up of body, soul and spirit. The body is viewed as a complex physical creation, the soul gives a human being personality, self-awareness and rationality, and the spirit is used to connect with God.

The Holy Trinity by German artist Albrecht Dürer.

STORIES OF GODS AND MEN

A fresco by Ambrogio Bergognone in the main apse of Saint Simpliciano church in Milan, showing the Holy Trinity.

Tripartite God of Christianity

VISHNU AND HIS AVATARS
INDIA

The Hindu pantheon revolves around three key gods: Brahma, the Creator; Vishnu, the Sustainer; and Shiva, the Destroyer.

All Hindu gods are effectively an expression of Brahman (not to be confused with Brahma), a single genderless supreme force. The word avatar comes from a Sanskrit word meaning 'descent' and refers to a deity manifesting in an earthly form. Hindu gods can have many avatars.

Dashavatara refers to the avatars of Vishnu. The list varies according to the way the religion is practised in different regions, but the standard list of avatars is as follows:

> **Matsya** (fish);
> **Kurma** (turtle);
> **Varaha** (boar);
> **Narasimha** (half man/half lion);
> **Vamana** (dwarf);
> **Parashurama** (warrior with axe);
> **Rama** (prince and king);
> **Krishna** (eighth son of Devaki and Vasudev);
> **Buddha** (founder of Buddhism);
> **Balarama** (Krishna's brother takes the ninth spot in some accounts);
> **Kalki** ('Eternity' or 'White Horse').

Rama and Krishna both hold prominent places in Hindu worship, despite not being gods themselves but avatars of Vishnu. Every time dharma, the path of righteousness, is threatened, Vishnu sends one of his avatars from his home, Vaikuntha, to earth to do battle on his behalf, and restore the balance of the world.

Vishnu's boar avatar, Varaha, saved the world from a great flood by retrieving the earth from the bottom of the seas. Vishnu's fish avatar, Matsya, warned Manu, the first human, that a flood was coming so that he was able to save himself.

Kalki is said to be the final avatar of Vishnu who will appear at the end of Kali Yuga, the current cycle of the world, to destroy all evil. As the harbinger of the end of time, he will appear on a white horse with a blazing sword.

An elaborate stela of the god Vishnu shows him at the centre. The left panel is topped by a figure of Brahma and right by Shiva.

STORIES OF GODS AND MEN

A sculpture of Vishnu Dashavatara with the ten avatars stands at the wall of Munneswaram Kovil Temple in Sri Lanka.

An amulet box depicting Vishnu travelling through a cosmic sphere on the legendary bird, Garuda.

Another avatar of Vishnu is a snake wrapped around Mount Meru and balanced on a turtle; the Hindu gods used this to churn the Ocean of Milk and produce amrita, the nectar of everlasting life. The gods hold one end of the snake and the demons hold the other, when the amrita is ready, the two parties fight over it, and the gods win.

One Hindu myth tells of a demon king, Hiranyakashipu, who has attained mortality and cannot be killed by man or beast. To solve this problem, Vishnu transforms into the avatar Narasimha, who is both half man and half lion, and so able to kill the demon king.

In between bouts of creation, Vishnu sleeps and rests on a multi-headed snake called Shesha, leader of the nagas, a race of snake-like beings, while having his feet massaged by his wife. Shesha was said to be Vishnu's most devoted follower.

Vishnu and his avatars

The dying god
Greece

In general, mythologies do not accept that death is the end.

While gods can be killed, they usually pass through to the underworld or the afterlife, with the added bonus of potential resurrection.

Greek gods do not die in the traditional sense, but are banished to Hades, the underworld, until their bodies have enough power to re-form.

For a Greek god to truly die, the elements they represent must cease to be significant. For Zeus, this can only happen if the sky and lightning are no longer acknowledged as significant by mankind. This has happened to two Greek gods only.

Pan is the god of nature and shepherds, with the body of a man and the legs of a goat. Reports of his death date back to the reign of Emperor Tiberius (AD14–37). According to the Greek historian Plutarch, a mysterious voice announced Pan's death to a returning sailor who brought the news from the island of Paxi. One theory behind Pan's death is symbolic of a shift from the pagan worship of the natural world to monotheism. It is also suggested that his death is related to the spread of Christianity.

Zeus is suspicious of the art of healing and, particularly, the prospect of his enemies coming back to life. So Zeus kills Asclepius, god of medicine and healing, with his thunderbolt after he heals an old enemy that Zeus had killed. It is said that Asclepius is later brought back from the dead.

A bronze sculpture of Pan by Italian artist Andrea Briosco (1470–1532).

Relief portraying Asclepius healing a youth, Piraeus Archaeological Museum, Greece.

STORIES OF GODS AND MEN

The dying god

Judaeo-Christian God
Middle East

The term Judaeo-Christian groups together Judaism and Christianity, due to the recognized parallels and commonalities in the two faith systems.

A Christian depiction of Abraham by Caravaggio. In this picture, the angel of the Lord intervenes to stop Abraham from completing the sacrifice of his son Isaac, instead indicating that he should sacrifice a nearby ram caught in the thickets.

The term 'Abrahamic religions' includes Islam in addition to Judaism and Christianity, as they all accept the tradition that God revealed himself to the prophet Abraham.

In all Abrahamic religions, God is seen as the creator and as being eternal, omnipotent and omniscient. He is also transcendent, meaning he exists outside of space and time, and therefore is not subject to anything located within his creation.

'Incorporeal' means without a physical body, presence or form, and is how God is referred to in Abrahamic religions. God is a supreme being, wholly independent of the material universe, beyond all physical laws, and cannot be affected by anything.

The Bible states that God is immutable and cannot change; the very nature of his divinity means that if he cannot change, he also cannot die. Also, this Judaeo-Christian God is referred to as 'wholly other' with completely different needs and functions from humans. Death, as a biological function of humans, does not apply to God.

Abraham's journey from Ur to the promised land of Canaan is one of the key features shared across the three modern Abrahamic faiths.

The "Tomb of Abraham" cenotaph, traditionally considered to be the burial place of Abraham and Sarah, in the Cave of the Patriarchs in Hebron, Palestine.

An Islamic depiction of Ibrahim's sacrifice (Abraham in the Hebrew Bible) from the Timurid Anthology, 1410-11.

Judaeo-Christian God

THE SKY FATHER
WORLD MYTHOLOGIES

There is a recurring concept in mythology of a sky god, addressed as father, to complement an earth mother. A masculine sky god is usually king of the gods, taking the position of the patriarch within a pantheon of gods.

In ancient Semitic mythology, sky god El and sky goddess Asherah rule the sky together.

In Maori mythology, Ranginui is the sky father and Papatuanuku the earth mother. In the beginning, there is only Io (or Iho), the timeless Supreme Being who created the universe. Io lived alone and inactive, with darkness and water. In order to become active, Io creates Papatuanuku, or simply Papa, and Ranginui (or Rangi). The sky father and the earth mother come together in the darkness and have seventy male children who become the Maori gods, but live squashed in the middle of their parents' embrace.

All of the sons, with the exception of Tawhiri Matea, the god of wind and storms, decides it would be best to separate their parents,

Zion National Park in Utah. The Navajo peoples of this land believe that Father Sky and Mother Earth work together to create an essential harmony between heaven and earth, providing the conditions needed for survival.

A Maori carving depicting Ranginui, the sky father and Papatuanuku, the earth mother holding each other in a tight embrace on a pataka (food storehouse) completed in the 1870s in New Zealand.

Jupiter, the sky father of Roman religion and mythology. The Ancient Romans also subscribed to the idea of a sky father.

A statuette of El, the supreme god of the Canaanite religion and the Mesopotamian Semites.

so they do not continue to live in darkness. The sons try, but Papa and Rangi's bond is too strong. The final son, Tane-Mahuta, is as strong as a kauri tree. He places his shoulders against Io and his feet against Rangi, pushes as hard as he can, and finally separates father sky and mother earth. The sons see the light of day for the first time and they are all happy, with the exception of Tawhiri Matea, who flees to the sky to join his father. Tawhiri Matea still causes storms to this day, in revenge for his brothers' acts.

To the Navajo people, in Native American mythology, Father Sky and Mother Earth represent male and female equally providing all we need to survive. The holy people create Father Sky and Mother Earth in perfect harmony and to complement each other. Mother Earth is nourished and energized by Father Sky and all earthly creations flourish. However, Mother Earth becomes boastful and proud, imagining that everything flourishing on earth is caused by her. Father Sky doesn't like what he hears and insists that he too is involved. She doesn't agree, they fall out and decide not to work together any more.

Without Father Sky's help, Mother Earth changes; the seasons change, volcanoes erupt, the water becomes polluted and the vegetation and animals die. After four years, the holy people convince Mother Earth to apologize and she sends the only surviving bird to Father Sky with the message. Father Sky accepts the apology and Mother Earth is restored. Their differences are settled and everyone agrees that everything in heaven and on earth is equal.

The sky father

Shamanism

Soyot shamanism
Siberia

The word *shaman* comes from one of the languages of the original Siberian tribes. When a community faces problems such as illness, they call upon their shamans to connect with the spirit world.

Although there are significant differences between the shamans of different religions, there are enough similarities to justify considering them together in the category of Siberian shamanism. As well as in Siberia proper, Siberian shamanism is found in surrounding areas such as northern China and the northern islands of Japan.

The Soyots are one branch of Siberian shamanism who lived mainly in the Okinsky district of Buryatia in Russia. One characteristic of Siberian shamanism is the special ritual costumes the shamans wear with images of the spirit helpers on them. The Soyot shamans of southern Siberia attach hundreds of textile snakes and ribbons to their costumes.

Siberian shamans play big flat drums. They dance and sing, and the heavy costumes and drums soon exhaust them. Fatigue helps them to enter the trance state very deeply to seek the spirit helpers. The Soyots are characterized by reindeer hunting and breeding. The shamans of those nomadic people guard a sacred alliance between the migrating reindeer and the ancestor spirits of the taiga, or boreal forest. In the Eveny midsummer ritual, Soyot shamans act out flying into the sky on reindeers.

Classical Siberian shamanism ended in the early 20th century. A campaign to stop seeking the advice of shamans was launched in 1917, following the Russian Revolution. Under Stalin, any remaining practising shamans were killed or imprisoned. Very few original artefacts survive, but there are some original costumes and drums in museums. Many indigenous people have gone back to the traditional practice of shamanism since the end of the Soviet era.

A Tungus Shaman in costume with a drum.

A shaman in the Coafan region, Ecuador, boils leaves for their psychoactive properties as used in ayahuasca.

Amazonian/Peruvian shamanism
Amazon basin/Peru

Shamans in Peru and the Amazon Basin use hallucinogenic plants and plant concoctions to achieve an altered state of consciousness that they believe allows them to travel between the worlds of gods and men, seeking advice from their spirit helpers.

San Pedro (*Trichocereus pachanoi*) is the sacred cactus and visionary 'teacher plant' of the South Americas, especially connected with shamans in the Peruvian Andes. San Pedro is named after Saint Peter, who holds the keys to Heaven, hinting at its ability to open the gates to other worlds.

Ayahuasca is an Amazonian plant mixture that is brewed and drunk as a tea, and its hallucinogenic effects last from four to eight hours. It is also called 'la purga' as it purges the body and induces a state of rebirth. Peruvians who specialize in the use of ayahuasca are known as 'Ayahuasqueros'.

Shamans in Peru and the Amazon Basin are also regarded as healers. They have healing altars comprising a complex arrangement of sacred objects that help them commune with the spirit world.

Celtic shamanism
Britain

The ancient Celts also practised shamanism. Stories such as 'Taliesin' and 'Amergin' contain references to shamanic spiritual journeys and rituals. Those stories and poems are dated to the 7th century.

Ancient Celtic warriors dressed for battle, with a shaman, c.1800.

The Celtic shaman's cosmos consists of three 'worlds': the upper, the lower, and the middle. These worlds are connected by the great tree of life; its roots lie in the lower world, its trunk extends through the middle world, where people live, to the upper world, where its branches hold the sun, the moon and the stars.

The Celtic shaman climbs up and down the tree, sometimes depicted as a ladder or pole, to gain access to the gods and spirits in the upper world and to visit the stag-headed lord of the underworld. These shamans are known as 'walkers between the worlds'.

Shape-shifting is an integral part of ancient Celtic shamanism. Both Irish shaman Amergin and the Welsh shaman Taliesin have the ability to take on the shape of another person, animal or object.

In shamanic traditions, everybody is guarded and watched over by a totem beast that joins them at the time of their birth and stays with them throughout their life. In addition, from time to time the shamans need to summon other

STORIES OF GODS AND MEN

animals when necessary, for example, to employ their speed, cunning or strength.

Celtic shamanism is seen as the precursor to Druidry, Saxon wizardry, magic, witchcraft and wicca. It recognizes the dark and dangerous sides of the spirit and capacity of humans, and identifies the need for allies – guides and guardians from the spirit world – to help the shaman's work. For example, a shaman may work with a salmon, using shape-shifting skills to turn into the fish and learn about its life; in exchange, the spirit salmon will learn something about shamanism.

In the story of Taliesin, the goddess Ceridwen leaves a young boy, Gwion, in charge of her cauldron, where she is preparing a liquid to guarantee knowledge and wisdom. Gwion falls asleep and when he awakes the fire is raging. While tending to the fire, some drops of liquid land on him and he absorbs all the wisdom that had been intended for Ceridwen's son. Gwion runs away and, furious, Ceridwen chases after him. He uses his new-found power to transform into many different animals, but the goddess transforms herself into the animal's nemesis and continues to chase him. Finally, Gwion transforms himself into a grain of wheat and Ceridwen turns herself into a hen and eats him – later she becomes pregnant. Knowing that Gwion is still alive inside of her, Ceridwen realises the child she is carrying is Gwion and decides to kill the infant when he is born. However, when she gives birth to beautiful baby boy she can't bear to kill him, so she casts him out to sea in a leather bag. A fisherman's son finds the bag and opens it to reveal the child inside. The boy says his name is Taliesin and spouts forth an endless stream of wisdom, poetry and philosophy. He grows up in the fisherman's hut to become a famous shaman and bard, and later serves in the court of King Arthur.

Pagans and druids celebrate the autumn equinox at the ancient standing stones at Stonehenge in England. The world-famous landmark was produced by a culture that left no written records and is thought to date back to 2600BC. To this day, a number of myths surround the origin of these enormous stones.

Shamanism

Medicine people
North America

In Native American culture the Medicine People are traditional healers and ritualists with several different names, depending on their region and religion.

Many Native Americans find the terms 'shaman' and 'shamanism' offensive. Western society has long used 'shaman' and 'medicine man' interchangeably to describe the holy men and women of Native America. There are hundreds of Indian nations in North America, each with its own culture, language and belief system, but their religious figures, medicine men and healers do not describe themselves as shamans.

Shamanism continues to be associated with a trance-like, mind-altering journey, which is not a major part of Native American cultures. A shaman is a specialist and master of this ecstatic journey and the term is not a synonym for a tribal healer, holy man or medicine man.

The Navajo medicine man (*hataii*) uses crystal rocks while chanting and shaking his hands. He selects a particular type of chant depending on the ailment. There are around sixty of these chants. Apprentices learn from their elders, and it takes many years to learn to perform these ceremonies, many medicine men specialize in only a few rituals. The medicine man believes that physical nature can be brought under control. The ceremonies and rituals involve communicating with certain spirits, but without entering the spirit world or summoning the gods.

The medicine man is believed to have a spiritual connection with animals and nature, with spirits inhabiting rivers, lakes, mountains, trees, flowers, plants, animals and birds.

An illustration by Bohuslav Kroupa of Navajo Indians, specifically 'Parushapats', encamped on the plains of Arizona c.1880s. It depicts a 'Jugwewagunt' (medicine man) reciting a legend.

The Native Americans believe that illness occurs when a bad spirit has entered the body and it is the medicine man's duty to disarm and remove this bad spirit with chants. The medicine man is often able to perform various forms of prophecy. In certain nations, such as the Sioux and the Cheyenne, the medicine man has the role of head warrior or war chief, making him the most influential man in the tribe.

In the Cherokee nation, the medicine man is considered the chosen one, with knowledge passed down for thousands of years. This tribe is one of the first to have set down their knowledge in written form, although often in code or written backwards to prevent other people from discovering their secrets.

A medicine man of the Mandan tribe in North Dakota in the costume of the Dog Dance.

Shamanism

SHAMANS OF THE DOGON
MALI

In central Mali, Western Africa, shamans of the Dogon tribe, both male and female, claim to be able to communicate with the head deity, Amma, who advises them on healing and divination practices.

European settlers referred to those traditional healers in a derogatory manner as 'witch doctors'. The Dogon are best known for religious ceremonies that include elaborate masks, costumes and dancing. The Dogon continue to live today as they have for thousands of years: on sandy plains below the Bandiagra cliffs in mud-brick houses.

They believe that the spirits of their ancestors exist among them, intervening in their lives. When this intervention causes problems, it is the shaman's role to mediate with the spirits through ritual.

The process of mastering shamanism is long and arduous, and begins with an initiation. A shaman is often chosen because he has survived grave illnesses – he is therefore seen to have cured himself with the aid of the spirits, a strong indicator of his suitability for shamanism.

Rock art has been discovered, dated to around 3300 BC, that shows representations of shamanic trance dances as well as monsters and spirit people. Most African tribes believe that God created the world and gave control to the spirits. The spirits take different forms, but are usually ancestral. Most believe that death and illness are not just caused by infections, but also dissatisfaction among the spirits with the ways of the living. It is considered important to keep the ancestors appeased and to respect them, and when there is conflict, it is the role of the shaman to settle them.

Because the shaman has a direct line of communication with the spirits, and deep respect from the community that maintains a strong connection to its ancestral spirits, the shaman maintains a position of power and prestige.

The Dogon believe that visitors from the star Sirius descended among them thousands of years ago. There is a claim that the Dogon once had a superior knowledge of astronomy, despite their not possessing astronomical equipment.

Dogon people in Mali in traditional religious dress.

STORIES OF GODS AND MEN

A samana warrior mask, used by the Dogon in ritual dances.

Shamanism

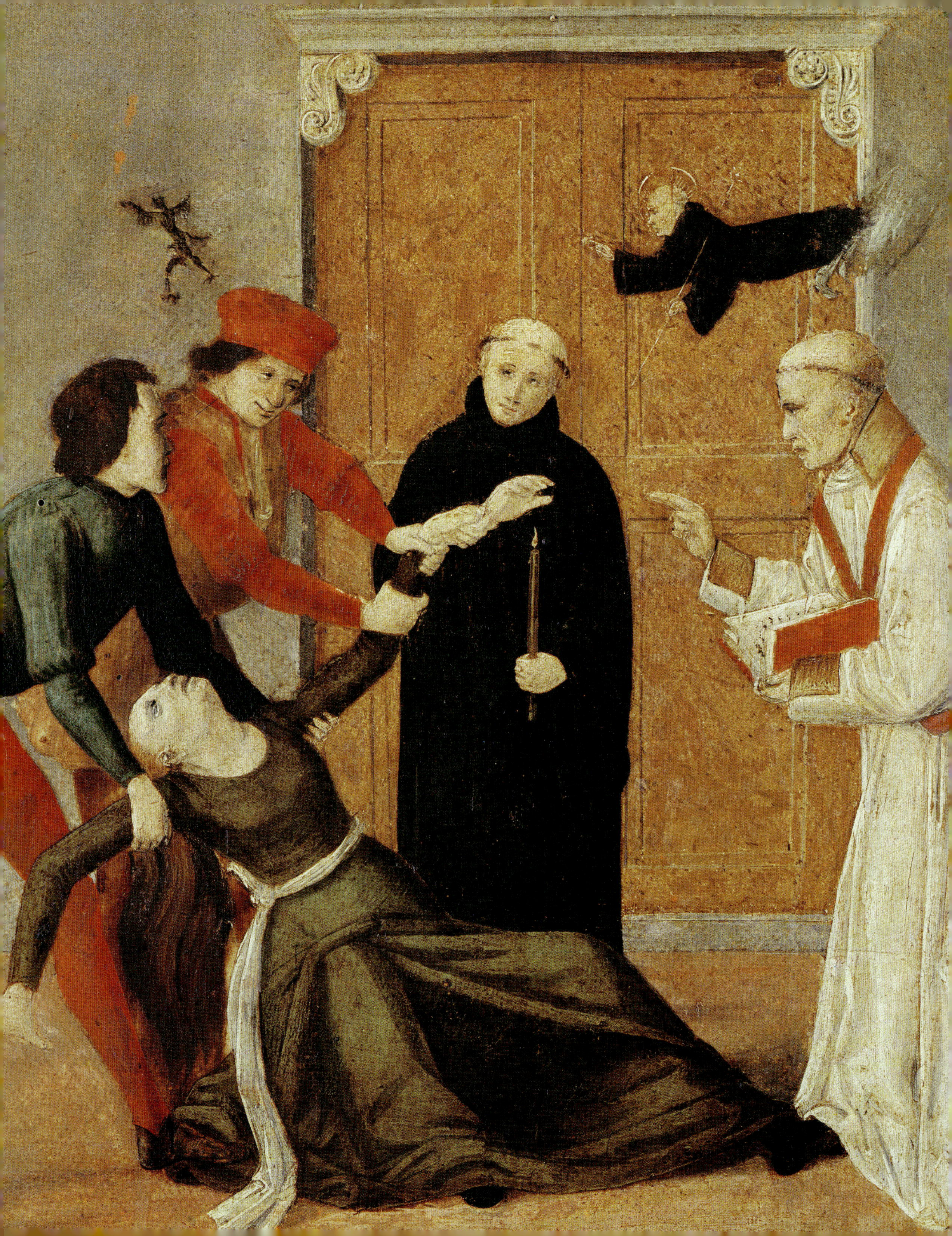

Legendary heroes and fantastical creatures and events

The shape-shifting involved in preparing for huge battles to the death or, more dramatically, the end of the world are in evidence with this set of characters. Malevolence is almost universally present, but there are some gentle narratives. In most cases we view beautiful immortal figures, terrifying monsters and exotic creatures. It is likely that these layered narratives have evolved over generations of oral tradition. Their simple lessons still offer something relatable and universal regarding human nature for the modern reader.

Defeating the beast
Greece

Ancient Greek myth is full of stories of mortal men accomplishing amazing acts of heroism and vanquishing abominable monsters. These stories have lodged in the hearts and minds of audiences and endure to this day as tales that are recounted around the world.

Theseus and the Minotaur

Theseus was the great founding hero of Athens and was miraculously fathered by both the god Poseidon and Aegeus, the king of Athens. Most famously, he defeated the loathsome Minotaur – a monstrous half-man, half-bull who lived in a labyrinth on Crete, where it received a ritual sacrifice of young Athenian boys and girls. Fortunately, Ariadne, the daughter of the king of Crete, fell in love with Theseus and she agreed to help him if he promised to marry her. She gave him a ball of thread which he unravelled to trace his path through the labyrinth, and later escape. He surprised the Minotaur asleep in its lair and was able to overpower and kill it. The couple then sailed back to Athens, but, tragically, Theseus forgot to use a white sail on his boat to signal his success to his father. Grief-stricken by what he assumed was his son's demise, King Aegeus jumped into the sea, from then on named the Aegean.

Changing stories

Originally, the myths of Ancient Greece were passed down through an oral tradition of epic poems and hymns. The oldest known written sources are Homer's epic poems the *Iliad* and the *Odyssey*. Many centuries later, particular versions of Greek myths were immortalized in the great tragedies and comedies of the Hellenistic Age and, even later, by Plutarch and Pausanias in the time of the Roman Empire. This means that there are often many variations on the same story.

Geometric Art

One of the most fascinating sources of Ancient Greek myth are the visual motifs depicted on surviving samples of pottery from the Geometric period (c.900–800BC).

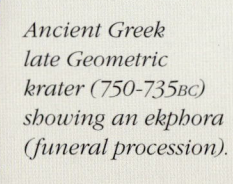

Ancient Greek late Geometric krater (750-735BC) showing an ekphora (funeral procession).

LEGENDARY HEROES AND FANTASTICAL CREATURES AND EVENTS

Perseus with the Head of Medusa, *by Benvenuto Cellini.*

PERSEUS AND MEDUSA

Perseus was the son of Danaë and the god Zeus. Perseus' grandfather, King Acrisius, received a premonition from the oracle that his grandson would one day kill him, so mother and baby were both exiled. When Perseus was grown, Danaë was pressured to marry King Polydectes against her will. Polydectes only agreed to leave Danaë alone if young Perseus succeeded in killing the one mortal Gorgon, Medusa – a grotesque monster with snakes for hair and the power to turn people to stone with her gaze. Perseus sought divine assistance and achieved numerous enchanted articles, which famously included winged sandals and a polished shield – a useful item to reflect the monster's gaze. With these he was able to kill Medusa and win his mother's freedom. In an ironic twist, Perseus did unwittingly fulfil his grandfather's prediction by killing Acrisius accidentally in a discus competition. Later, Perseus fathered his own son, Electryon, the grandfather of Heracles.

Defeating the beast

Heracles

There are many stories from Ancient Greece of heroes overcoming impossible challenges and achieving super-human feats, but Heracles (later known as Hercules by the Romans) was Greece's most famous hero renowned for his outstanding strength. A crucial aspect of his character was his remorse and sorrow for his past actions: he had been manipulated by the goddess Hera to lose his mind and murder his wife and children. Upon waking, Heracles' first desire was to kill himself. Instead, he sought atonement for his crimes. He received his punishment via the oracle at Delphi which involved the penance of serving King Eurystheus by performing twelve labours, each an impossible feat. With help from the deities Hermes and Athena, Heracles completed the tasks over the next twelve years. These included killing a lion no weapon had ever wounded; killing the nine-headed creature Hydra; entering both the lower world and the vaults of heaven; and cleansing the Augean stables in a single day – finding thousands of cattle and accumulated mess, he simply redirected two rivers to wash it clean.

Terracotta plaque (the so-called Campana plaque) depicting Heracles capturing the Cretan bull in Rome, Italy.

130   LEGENDARY HEROES AND FANTASTICAL CREATURES AND EVENTS

The 12 Labours of Heracles

1 Kill the Nemean Lion, whose hide was so strong that no arrow could pierce it.

2 Kill the evil, snake-like Lernean Hydra with nine heads.

3 Capture the Cerynian Hind, protected by the goddess Artemis.

4 Capture the deadly Erymanthian Boar.

5 Clean the Augean Stables that housed thousands of cows, and had not been cleaned in 30 years, in a single day.

6 Kill the murderous Stymphalian Birds, whose claws and beaks were sharp as metal and whose feathers flew like darts.

7 Capture the fire-breathing Cretan Bull.

8 Capture the bloodthirsty Horses of Diomedes who fed on human flesh.

9 Take the Girdle of the Amazon Queen Hippolyte.

10 Capture the Cattle of Geryon, a winged monster with three human bodies.

11 Take the Golden Apples of the Hesperides nymphs.

12 Capture Cerberus, the three-headed guard dog of the underworld.

Stone statue of Heracles.

Monkey
China

The Monkey King (Sun Wukong) is a Chinese mythological figure. It features in a body of legends that can be traced back to the period of the Song dynasty (960–1279). The Monkey King is a main character in *Journey to the West*, written by Wu Cheng'en in the 16th century.

From the beginning of time, a rock on the Mountain of Flowers and Fruit has been soaking up natural goodness and *qi* energy, a concept that denotes air or breath and combines the physical and the spiritual within a body. The rock releases a stone egg and from it hatches the Monkey King. This monkey is a high-spirited trickster who, after ruling for 400 years, wishes to learn the secret of immortality. He has learnt tricks from an immortal Taoist master, such as how to transform himself into different animals and how to use clouds to travel thousands of miles in a single somersault. In defiance of the Great Emperor of Jade, the monkey causes havoc in the heavens.

The heavenly authorities try to catch the monkey so they can punish him for this act of high treason. Finally, the heavenly army captures the monkey, but they cannot kill him. Instead, the Buddha traps him inside the great mountain Wu Zhi Shan. After 500 years, the monkey is rescued by a monk, who accompanies him to the West on a journey full of action and adventure. The monk collects holy scriptures in the West and carries them back for the Buddha, and by accompanying the monk, the Monkey King atones for his crimes and earns enlightenment. In *Journey to the West*, the Monkey King carries a magical iron rod that can change size. Obtained from the Dragon King of the Eastern Sea, the rod weighs several tons, but can be kept behind the monkey's ear. The character of the Monkey King embodies the Buddhist concept of *monkey mind*, representing the restlessness of the human spirit.

The Monkey King (Sun Wukong), a main character in the novel Journey to the West *written by Wu Cheng'en.*

LEGENDARY HEROES AND FANTASTICAL CREATURES AND EVENTS

A Japanese illustration of the Monkey King (Sun Wukong).

The adventures of Okuninushi
Japan

Okuninushi is a deity, or *kami* in Japanese Shinto. Originally, he is the ruler of Izumo Province, but then becomes ruler of an unseen world of spirits and magic.

A bronze statue of Okuninushi in Izumo-taisha, Japan.

The legend of the white hare of Inaba goes this way. Okuninushi has many brothers and they all treat him as they would a servant. The brothers hear of a beautiful princess (or goddess) and decide that they all want to ask for her hand in marriage. They go to meet her, taking Okuninushi with them to carry their heavy baggage. Before long he is lagging behind. When the brothers come across a hare that has been stripped of its fur and is in pain, they give the hare bad advice and cause its pain to worsen. When Okuninushi finds the hare he tends its wounds and soon it is completely healed.

The hare makes a prediction that Princess Yagakami will fall in love with Okuninushi, rather than one of his brothers, even though he looks like a servant. The prediction comes true and the brothers are enraged. They make repeated attempts to kill Okuninushi, but his mother saves him every time. Eventually, his

Statue of the Hare of Inaba and Okuninushi in Japan.

Izumo-taisha is one of the most ancient and important Shinto shrines in Japan. According to legend, when Ninigi-no-Mikoto, grandson of the Sun Goddess Amaterasu, descended from the heavens, Okuninushi granted Izumo province to him. Amaterasu was much pleased by this action and she presented Izumo-taisha to Okuninushi.

mother tells him to run away and he flees to the underworld. There he falls in love with Suseri-Hime, the daughter of the storm god Susanoo. The storm god does not approve and tries to kill Okuninushi. After Okuninushi survives several attempts on his life, Susanoo begins to admire him. One night, Okuninushi ties Susanoo's hair to the rafters and escapes with his daughter, to become ruler of Izumo province.

Okuninushi builds and rules the world until the arrival of Ninigi-no-Mikoto, the grandson of Amaterasu, a major deity of the Shinto religion. Okuninushi hands over political control to Ninigi, but retains control of religious and spiritual affairs.

In Japanese folklore, Okuninushi is the god of farming, medicine, healing and marriage.

Koschei the Deathless
Russia

Koschei the Deathless, also known as Koshchey the Immortal, is an evil sorcerer and shape-shifter in Slavic folklore. Depicted as an ugly man who rides naked on his enchanted horse through the mountains of Russia, he has power over the elements, much as his female counterpart, Baba Yaga, does. As a shape-shifter he can appear as a monster or a human, and takes the form of a whirlwind to kidnap his female victims.

The Legend of Koschei and Prince Ivan is told in this form: Prince Ivan's parents die and his sisters all marry and leave him alone. Ivan feels lonely and sets off to find his sisters. Along the way, he meets and falls in love with Marya the warrior. After they marry, Marya decides to go to war; she leaves Ivan in charge of the house, with strict instructions not to look in a certain closet, but he cannot resist. He finds an old man there, bound with twelve chains. The old man begs for water and Ivan, being a kind soul, brings him twelve buckets of water.

On drinking the water, the old man's powers are restored, he regains his youthful strength and is able to break free of his chains. This is Koschei, who disappears to find and kidnap Marya. Ivan attempts to follow, but Koschei chops him into pieces and throws him into the sea. Luckily, Koschei's sisters and their wizard husbands appear and save him. Ivan is reunited with Marya and together they defeat Koschei. Ivan's steed kicks Koschei in the head, and then the couple burn the body, proving that Koschei is not truly immortal.

In most versions, Koschei becomes immortal by removing his soul and hiding it inside different objects and animals that he locks in a chest. His soul is stored inside a needle, an egg, a duck, a rabbit, and all placed inside a chest that is buried under an oak tree. However, he has made a mistake when casting the spell, which proves his undoing.

Koshchei the Deathless – an illustration to the fairy tale Mariya Morevna.

Koschei the Deathless carrying off Maria Morevna, by the Russian artist Boris Zvorykin (1872–1942).

LEGENDARY HEROES AND FANTASTICAL CREATURES AND EVENTS

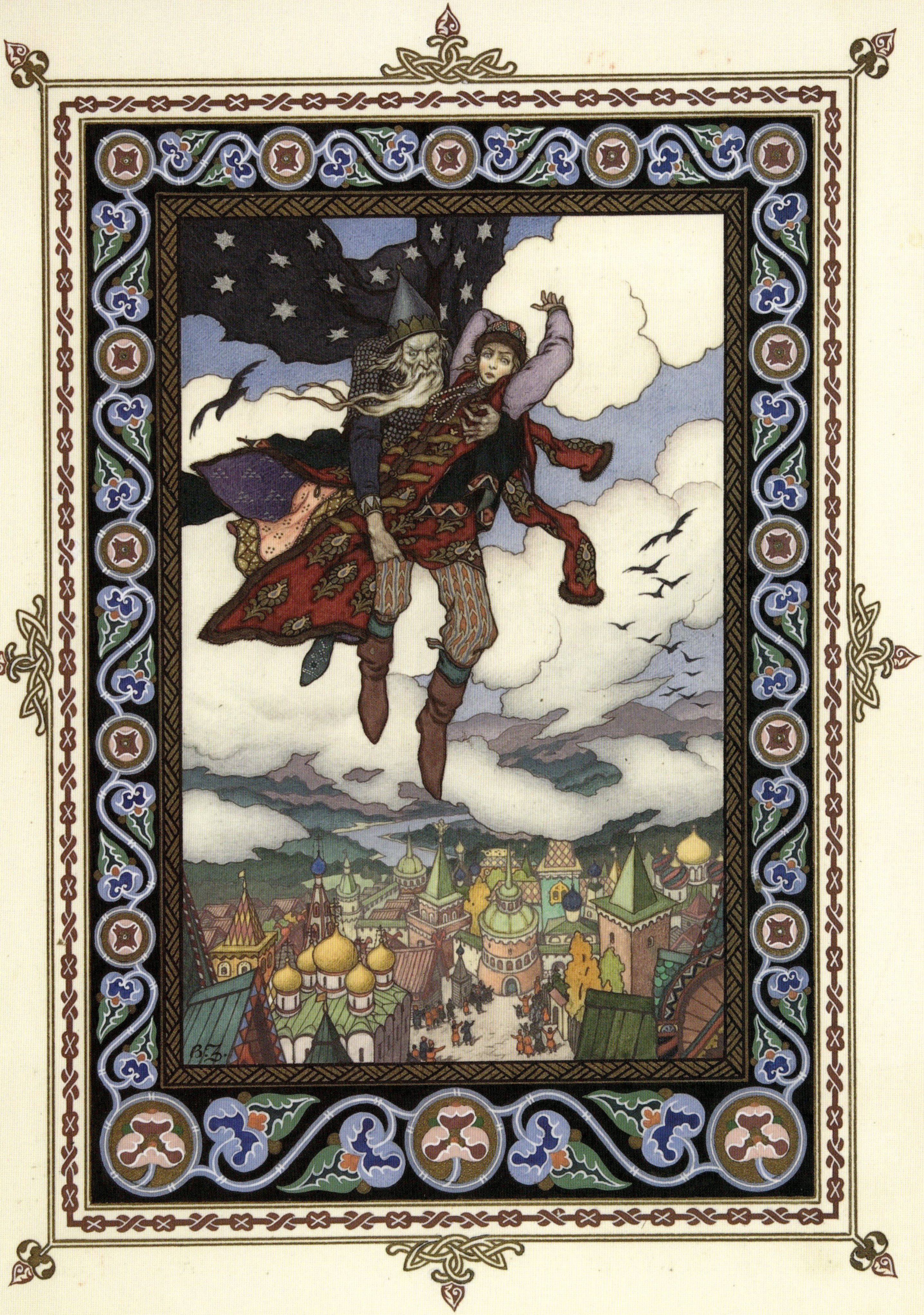

Vampires, demons and spirits
World mythologies

Vampires

A vampire is a being from folklore that feeds on the blood of the living. Older versions of the vampire tales describe these creatures as supernatural beings without human form. The modern idea of a vampire – a revenant, or undead – came about in the 18th century. Vampire legends originated in Eastern Europe and the Balkans, and particularly Transylvania. The most famous figure in vampire literature is that in Bram Stoker's *Dracula*, written in 1897 in the United Kingdom.

Some vampires are said to have no reflection, some can shape-shift, and some can be killed by sunlight. The only feature they have in common is the need to drink blood. Centuries ago, some people believed that you could recognize a vampire at birth – for example, a child born with an extra nipple (in Romania) or with a split lower lip (in Russia).

In medieval Europe, people did not understand the processes of decay and so when bodies were dug up, what were normal signs of decomposition could be wrongly interpreted. For example, intestinal decomposition could create bloating and force blood up into the mouth, making it look as though the corpse has recently sucked blood.

Vampires continue to appear widely in popular culture, and many people around the world have identified themselves as vampires belonging to Gothic-inspired subcultures.

Portrait of Vlad III the Impaler, or Dracula (1431-76) who inspired Bram Stoker's novel Dracula, *written in 1897. This anonymous painting is from the 16th century.*

LEGENDARY HEROES AND FANTASTICAL CREATURES AND EVENTS

A 14th-century Italian depiction of the exorcism of a demon from a possessed woman.

Demons

The name 'demon' derives from the Latin *daemonium*, meaning a thing of divine nature. Demons are generally regarded as malevolent. Some cultures, including Native American nations, consider destructive natural phenomena, including hurricanes and drought, to be demonic forces.

Names for demons include vampires, goblins, Satan, poltergeists, Loki, fallen angels and Gorgons. There are many accounts, across cultures and up to the present day, of demons who possess people and require exorcism.

Spirits

A spirit is a supernatural being, usually without physical form. Some cultures believe there to be a spiritual being living inside each one of us. This spiritual essence is eternal and the physical human body is only its temporary home.

The name *ghost* can sometimes be used in place of *spirit*, but tends to have negative connotations. Some people believe ghosts are earthbound spirits who have not yet gone into the light of the spirit world. Unlike the concept of the soul, which is eternal and exists before the body, a spirit develops and grows with the body, as an integral part of a human being.

God is called the Holy Spirit in Christian theology, but the Bible also mentions evil spirits.

Vampires, demons and spirits

PRINCE IGOR AND KRAK
RUSSIA AND POLAND

PRINCE IGOR

The Song of Igor's Campaign, a rhapsodic prose poem written in ancient Russian around 1187, tells of Prince Igor Svyatoslavich's expedition and battles. The elevated style and atmosphere of the work gave rise to a semi-mythological concept of a golden age of chivalry in Russia prior to the 13th-century Mongol invasion.

Prince Igor Svyatoslavich the Brave was a historical figure who lived from 1151 to 1202. He was a Russian prince, a member of the Rurik dynasty, with a successful military career.

However, in 1183 Ivor and his family were defeated by a nomadic tribe, the Cumans, and captured. In 1186, Ivor escaped from captivity and resumed his rule of Novgorod-Seversky, which is in modern-day Ukraine.

Prince Igor, an opera written in 1887 by Alexander Borodin, is based on the epic poem.

Igor Svyatoslavich's battle with the pechenegs (from the Radziwill Chronicle*), 15th century. Found in the collection of the Library of the Russian Academy of Sciences, St Petersburg.*

Krakus mound in Krakow, Poland.

KRAK

Krakus, or Krak, is a legendary Polish hero and founder of the ancient city of Krakow in the 8th century. In the legend, a town's people are living under the rule of an evil dragon, which dwells in a cave at the foot of Wawel Hill, by the River Vistula. The King calls for the dragon to be killed, and offers his daughter's hand in marriage as reward. Many knights try and fail to kill the dragon. Krak longs to marry the princess. What he lacks in weaponry he makes up for in ingenuity. He stuffs a sheep full of sulphur and leaves it outside the dragon's cave. The dragon eats the sheep, and the sulphur ignites in its belly. The dragon becomes so thirsty that it drinks half the river and bursts. Krak builds the city of Krakow and Wawel Castle on Wawel Hill, marries the King's daughter and becomes Prince Krak.

Later Prince Krak becomes King of Poland, and keeps the Roman armies at bay. To honour Krak in death, noblemen and peasants bring sand and earth to create a mountain with commanding views over the surrounding landscape. Known as Krakus Mound (Kopiec Krakusa), this feature remains to this day and gives panoramic views of the modern city of Krakow.

Dragons
World mythologies

Dragons are mythological beasts, usually depicted as fire-breathing monsters. In Western traditions they are generally described as enormous, scaly, four-legged creatures with bat-like wings and a long tail. In Eastern traditions they are usually wingless and tend to be more benign.

The earliest references to dragons are from Mesopotamia, in modern-day Iraq. The story of the dragon spread to ancient Greece, Japan and China. Dragon tales vary greatly across the world. In one Greek myth, bathing in dragon's blood brings invincibility. In Asia, the dragon is a royal symbol that brings good luck.

Dragons are often symbols of evil: for example, in Christianity the dragon represents paganism and sin. In many tales the destruction of a dragon marks the end of some heroic figure's personal quest. Such famous dragon fighters included Perseus, Thor, Beowulf, St George, Jason and Heracles.

In Chinese mythology, four Dragon-Kings rule the four seas. They are brothers, Ao Kuang, Ao Jun, Ao Shun and Ao Ch'in, who also have the power to bring forth rain and to cause rain to cease, and so were central in prayers in times of drought and flooding. At one time there were temples to the Dragon-Kings next to every well in China.

Dragons continue to feature in fantasy works, including films, books, video games and board games.

A 16th-century depiction of Saint George and the Dragon by Albrecht Dürer.

LEGENDARY HEROES AND FANTASTICAL CREATURES AND EVENTS

A 12th-century silk tapestry from Central Asia. The form of the dragon, with its long snout and its tail hooked behind its leg, represents a Tang Dynasty convention that survived in Central Asia until at least the Yuan dynasty.

Dragons 143

THE APOCALYPSE
WORLD MYTHOLOGIES

Throughout history, many people have believed that humankind will one day be destroyed by a global catastrophe – an apocalyptic event – just as such an event wiped out the dinosaurs. This idea of an apocalypse continues to be a potent one in our world.

The word derives from the ancient Greek term *apokalypsis*, meaning 'disclosure of knowledge'. The word in this context derives from the Book of Revelation, *Apokalypsis Ioannou* ('John's Revelation'), a part of the New Testament. Written by a mysterious figure sometimes referred to as John of Patmos, it describes his prophecy of how the world will end and so the word 'apocalypse' has come to mean both the revelation of impending doom and the catastrophic event itself.

The Great Day of His Wrath, engraved by Charles Mottram (1807–76), is a Christian depiction of the Apocalypse as predicted in the Bible.

In the 16th century, the French prophet Nostradamus (Michel de Nostredame) wrote about the end of the world in a letter to his son. His description was of worldwide floods and firestorms that would destroy everything but the weather and space. He believed the apocalypse would take place 7,000 years after he wrote the letter, in the year 8555. Cults have since sprung up that believe in this prophecy with total conviction.

The Mayan calendar appears to end in 2012, which led many people to believe that December 2012 would mark the end of the world. This was one of the few specific dates we have been given in the contemporary world. But as explained elsewhere, to the Maya this date represented the end of one cycle and the beginning of another.

In Norse mythology, Ragnarök is the doom and destruction of the gods, which sees the world destroyed by fire (see pages 146–7).

A portrait of Michel de Nostredame (Nostradamus) painted by his son César de Nostredame.

Four Horsemen of the Apocalypse
Middle East

The Four Horseman of the Apocalypse appear in the 6th revelation of the Book of Revelation. John's vision is that these figures on horseback will appear as destroyers and mark the end of time. The horses they ride are of different colours: red, black, white and pale green. The red horse represents war, the colour signifying bloodshed; this horseman carries a sword. The black horse represents famine resulting from war; this horseman carries a pair of scales. The pale green horse represents fear, sickness, decay and death, the colour conveying the sickly tinge of the dying or recently dead. The figure of the white horse, conquest, is the only one whose significance is debated. Some people say it represents Christ, who will ultimately conquer all. The rider will be crowned and will then set off to conquer the world.

The Apocalyptic Riders – a plate from a series of 21 woodcuts with scenes from the Apocalypse for Martin Luther's translation of the New Testament. Four editions were published in Augsburg by Silvan Otmar between March 1523 and April 1524.

The Apocalypse   145

RAGNARÖK
SCANDINAVIA

In Old Norse, Ragnarök means 'the fate of the gods'. It is the day of doom and apocalypse in Norse mythology. Some have described Ragnarök as being cyclical. The end of the world will be followed by new creation, time and time again, and it is this cycle that defines history, so creation and destruction are necessary to each other. Others have described Ragnarok as a one-off prediction.

An illustration of Ragnarök entitled Then the Awful Fight Began, *by George Wright. The image depicts the great battle which will result in the destruction of the gods of Norse mythology and the end of the world.*

A depiction of Ragnarök, the day of doom and apocalypse in Norse mythology.

The Valkyries are women in Norse mythology who decide who will live and who will die in battle. They transport the chosen few back to Valhalla, the hall of the chief god Odin. The brave warriors wait in Valhalla until the time of Ragnarök, when they are to battle against Fenrir, a giant wolf, son of Loki and enemy of Odin. Fenrir continues to grow, despite being captured and chained up by the gods, and by the time of Ragnarök his bulk has filled the entire space between heaven and earth.

Norse mythology predicts that the sun, the goddess Sol, will be devoured by Fenrir during the apocalyptic events of Ragnarök. Thor, son of Odin, once fought and lost his battle with his chief enemy, the Midgard Serpent, another of Loki's sons. They will meet again at Ragnarök and both will perish.

The warning signs that Ragnarök is approaching include three winters with no summer or sun in between, and then three roosters crowing in different locations: in the forest, in Valhalla, and in hell.

It is Odin's responsibility, as supreme among gods and men, to delay the day of doom for as long as possible. After Ragnarök, everything will be submerged in water. The earth will then reappear from under the seas.

The only humans who will survive Ragnarök are the Norse figures Lif and Lifthrasir, who will repopulate the world. Some of the Norse gods, led by the good god Balder, will be resurrected after the final battle of Ragnarök.

The Apocalypse

Shiva destroys the world
India

The Hindu pantheon revolves around three main gods known as the Trimurti: Brahma (the Creator), Vishnu (the Sustainer) and Shiva (the Destroyer).

Each of these gods has many avatars, or alternative earthly forms. Of all the gods in Hindu mythology, Shiva is the only one who can both save and destroy.

Shiva is the father of the elephant-headed god Ganesha. He rides the bull Nandi, which is also gatekeeper of the god's residence. He is also patron of yoga, meditation and the arts. Shiva and his beloved Parvati are represented in the Ardhanarisvara form (half male and half female icon) to symbolize equality between a man and a woman in a perfect marriage.

Other depictions of Shiva include a version with an extra eye on his forehead and a serpent around his neck. The serpent represents the ego that can be worn

Sculpture of the Trimurti from around the 8th century AD at the Kailasanatha temple in the Ellora Caves in Maharashtra, India.

This painting is part of a series illustration the 15-century Sanskrit love poem, the Rasamanjari *(Essence of the Experience of Delight), by Bhanudatta. In this scene, Parvati is pleading with her husband, Shiva, who has just cheated her out of a necklace in a game of chaupar.*

harmlessly if mastered. He is also shown as covered in ash – a warning against being too concerned with physical appearance.

Shiva is the Nataraja ('lord of dance') who performs the Lasya ('dance of creation') and the Tandav. The latter is performed at the end of every age to destroy the universe, and translates as 'the cosmic dance of death'.

According to legend, Shiva almost brings about the end of the world by mistake, by performing the Tandav before it is time. His first wife is Sati, but her father does not approve of the marriage and so she jumps into a fire and perishes. Shiva is meditating at the time but, when told of his wife's demise, starts the cosmic dance of death in his rage. The other gods who are present scatter Sati's ashes over him to calm him down, so he doesn't finish the dance. He then meditates for many years, until Sati is reborn as Parvati.

Shiva's destruction is not negative. It is a positive, nourishing destruction that leads to the transformation of the world. He destroys evil, ignorance and bad karma to ensure human improvement and spiritual progression.

In the end, when no more improvements are possible and humans have no inner conflict, Shiva will destroy death.

The Apocalypse

Return of the Spider Woman
North America

Spider Grandmother, also known as Spider Woman or Spider Old-Woman, is creator of the world in Native American mythology, including that of the Hopi people. The Hopi, also known as Moqui Indians, are associated with the land now named Arizona. Their full name is Hopituh Shi-nu-mu ('the peaceful people').

'Spider Rock' in Canyon de Chelly, Arizona, is the home of Spider Grandmother, who is also linked with dreamcatchers (a small decorated hoop, said to give its wearer good dreams). She spun a web that was covered in mountain dew; the web was thrown into the sky and created the stars at night.

A Kooyemsi hood from the Hopi tribe in Arizona. Traditional Hopi religious artifacts like these are a link to the unseen spiritual dimension of the Native American culture.

LEGENDARY HEROES AND FANTASTICAL CREATURES AND EVENTS

Grandmother Spider steals the sun

When the earth is brand new, there is no light or warmth for the people and animals of the world. Everything is in darkness. The sun is being guarded by the sun-keepers who kept it hanging over their tree. The animals hold a meeting about how they can get to the sun. First the beaver tries to steal the sun and hide it in his bushy tail; then the eagle tries to steal the sun and fly with it on his back. In both cases the sun is too hot and begins to burn them, so they drop it on the ground where the sun-keepers find it and return it to their tree. Grandmother Spider spins a web from her village to the sun and brings the sun back on her web. Then she spins another web from her village to the sky, takes the sun and leaves it in the sky for all to enjoy and benefit from.

The Hopis believe there have been three previous worlds that were all destroyed by humanity's ruinous practices. The current one is identified as the fourth world, and will soon transition into a fifth. At the end of each world, Spider Grandmother leads the Hopi and other good people into the next incarnation or phase through a tunnel that symbolizes the womb.

Grandmother Spider continues to weave the web of life throughout every cycle of creation. Humanity is linked by this web; not as separate beings, but by sharing the same energy. Each occupies a part in the great mystery.

Spider Rock in Apache County, Arizona.

The Apocalypse

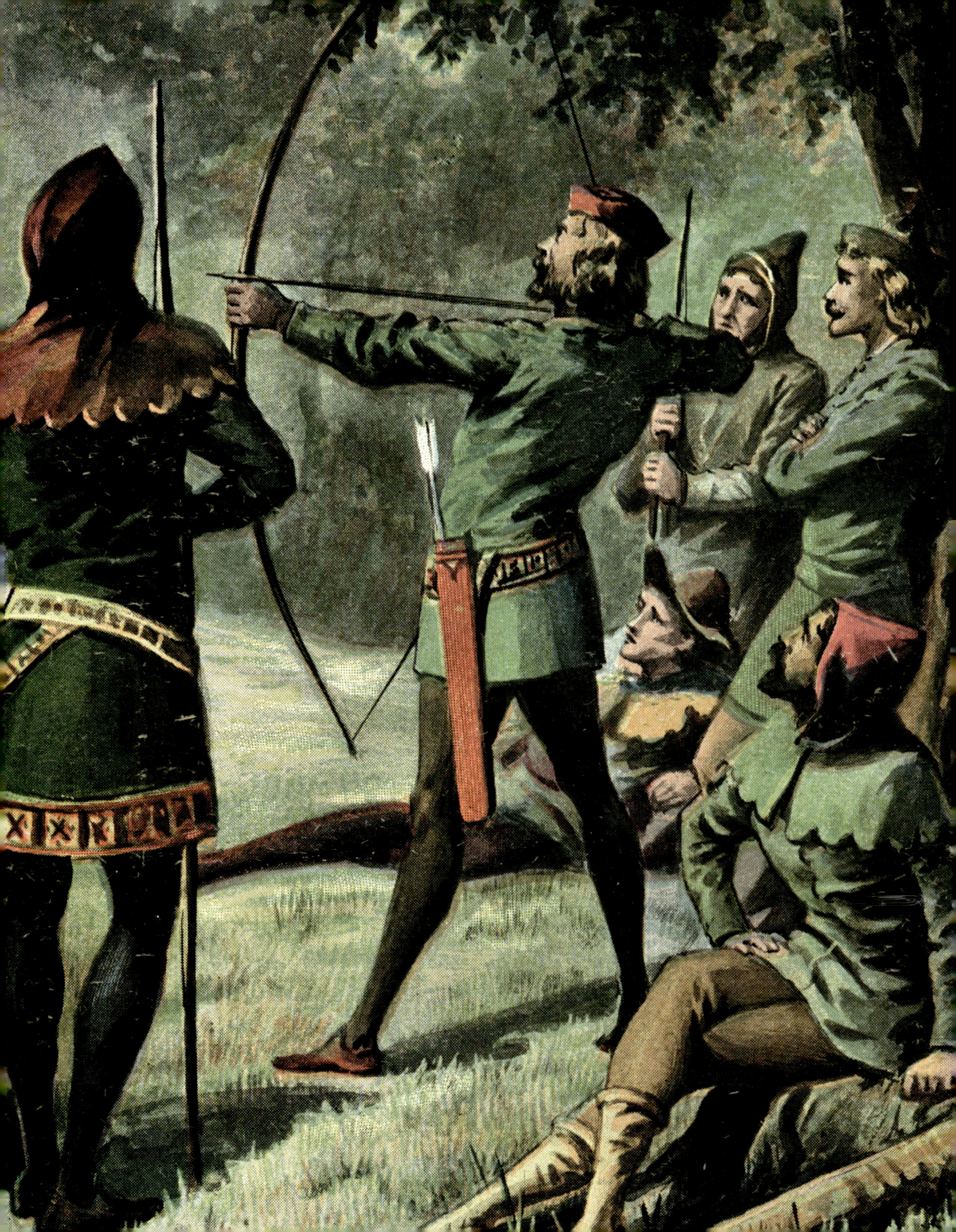

TRICKSTERS

The figure of the trickster appears in many world mythologies. They are quick-witted and disruptive of the social order. Tricksters can be gods or mortals and their actions can have huge consequences for all. When monotheistic religions were formed, with a concept of truth at their core, the trickster became less desirable and more devilish.

COYOTE AND RAVEN
NORTH AMERICA

Coyote and Raven, two key tricksters in Native American mythology, share many traits. Across the tribes, a wide variety of tales and legends are told about each. Coyote is the first being to tell a lie and thus introduces sickness and death to the world. An argument between Coyote and Wolf ends with Wolf killing Coyote's son, marking the first death.

When the moon goes missing, Coyote offers to take its place. From this viewpoint he can spy on everyone. After a while, the people vote him out of the sky as they are tired of his storytelling. In anger, he throws one of his eyeballs so high in the sky that it gets stuck and becomes the star Arcturus. Thus, Coyote can continue to spy on everyone.

Another tale tells how Coyote brings fire to the world's beings. He steals the fire from three sisters who are guarding it at the top of a mountain. Working with other creatures in the forest, he transfers it stage by stage until it reaches the wood. Coyote teaches the

The coyote was described by European colonialists as a 'Spanish fox' or 'jackal'. Its behavioural qualities were interpreted by indigenous Americans as being associated with intelligence and adaptability, coupled with an untrustworthy nature.

people how to get fire out of wood by rubbing sticks together so they can cook and will never be cold again.

Raven has a dual role in folklore through creation and mischief. According to some legends, Raven's droppings become mountains and so he creates the land. He then discovers the first people inside a clam shell and frees them into the world. While Native American tribes believe Raven holds the key to open many of life's treasures, they also realize that his actions are always made for selfish reasons.

One old man is hoarding all the light in the world. Raven disguises himself as a baby and tricks his way into the house, where he is given a bag of stars to play with. He then flies out of the house with the light. When Eagle tries to steal the bag, some of the light falls out and becomes the moon and the stars.

A traditional Aztec illustration of Coyote.

A raven surveys the landscape in Utah. In Native American mythology, it is known for its mischievous nature.

Coyote and Raven

Anansi
Ghana

Anansi (also known as Ananse and Kwaku Ananse) is a trickster spider-god who can also take the form of a human and other animals. West Africans believe Anansi to be the creator of the world. Elsewhere, he is credited with persuading Nyame, the god of the Akan people of Ashanteland, to give the people both rain and night.

A wooden staff finial of Ananse the Spider in gold leaf from 1900.

A giant whip scorpion spider (Damon medius) from Ghana. This ancient order of arachnid may well have been the inspiration for Anansi.

While Anansi is sometimes seen as wise and helpful to humans, he is more often viewed as a cunning trickster with few scruples who takes advantage of others. However, it is his ability to use cunning to outwit creatures bigger and more powerful than himself that made stories of Anansi popular during times of mass slavery.

Spider stories

In a world with no stories, Anansi goes to the sky god Nyame in an attempt to get his box of precious tales and bring them to the people. Nyame states that the only way that he will give Anansi the box is if Anansi brings him Onini the python, Osebo the leopard, Mmoboro the hornet and Mmoatia the invisible fairy. Anansi uses trickery to capture all these creatures, takes them to Nyame and, in return, brings stories to the world.

Reynard the fox
Europe

The three animals that appear most often in European folklore are the fox, the wolf and the bear, the primary forest carnivores. Reynard is a trickster fox in north-west European literature (French: Renart, German: Reineke, Latin: Renartus, Dutch: Reinaert). Stories involving Reynard show him using his cunning to get the better of stronger animals. His main enemy is his uncle, the wolf Ysengrin. Written during the Middle Ages, the Reynard stories are considered at one level to be a satire on politics, religion and the aristocracy. The first poem in which Reynard appears was written around 1150 in Latin by the poet Nivardus, in Ghent, and was entitled *Ysengrimus*. The first story known was written around 1170 in old French by Pierre de Saint-Cloud and entitled *Le Roman de Renart*.

Reynard the Fox wearing a mitre, preaching to the geese and other birds, France c.1300–40

Wolf and Fox Hunt *by Rubens (1577–1640)*.

Reynard's treasure

The animals complain to King Noble the Lion about Reynard's trickery, and so the King decides to bring the fox before the court to answer for his crimes. The King sends Bruin the Bear to fetch Reynard, but the fox tricks the bear, which gets its head stuck inside a log searching for honey. Bruin is then attacked by humans and loses his ears. Next, the King sends Tybalt the Cat to bring Reynard to justice, but the fox tricks the cat into a trap meant for him. Finally, Grymbart the Badger succeeds in bringing Reynard to the court of the King. Reynard tells the King that all the other animals have plotted against him in order to steal his hidden treasure. The King frees Reynard so that the fox can show him where the treasure is hidden, but instead Reynard escapes.

CROW
AUSTRALIA

Australian Aborigines have incorporated into their folklore plant or animal totems – or emblems with spiritual significance – in order to control and protect their environment. These animal totems are their spiritual siblings. Aborigines regard Crow and Eagle as two 'moiety' birds (and ancestors) in that they represent two aspects of a greater whole. Crow is the trickster whereas Eagle is a more sombre figure.

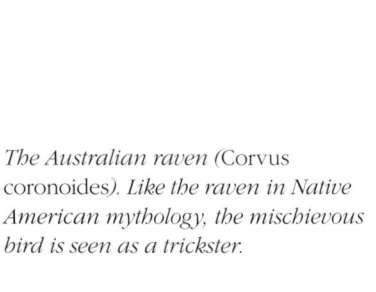

*The Australian raven (*Corvus coronoides*). Like the raven in Native American mythology, the mischievous bird is seen as a trickster.*

In the Dreamtime (see page 20-1) Crow figures as a sacred and spiritual bird that carries the spirits of the dead across the water. He is also the bringer of fire.

Seven Karatgurk sisters on the Yarra River guard the secret of fire in the coals that they carried on their digging sticks, but Crow finds a way to trick them and

The Pleiades, or 'Seven Sisters' in the constellation of Taurus are said to be the Karatgurk sisters.

take fire to the people. He buries snakes under a mound of earth and tells the sisters they should dig for food there. As they dig the snakes become angry and attack the sisters, who try to fight them off with their digging sticks. In the process, some coals fly off from the digging sticks; Crow collects them and flies up to the top of a tree. Soon lots of birds have crowded round Crow demanding to know the secret of fire. In the chaos, Crow drops some coals and starts a bushfire. The fire burns all Crow's white feathers to black, and the Karatgurk women are swept away into the sky, where they become the star cluster Pleiades.

Yarra River in Victoria, Australia. The Karatgurk sisters lived along the banks of this river, guarding the secret of fire before Crow caused the great bushfire.

ROBIN HOOD
BRITAIN

Robin Hood is a heroic outlaw and archer in English folklore who steals from the rich and gives to the poor. Some believe the character is based on a real outlaw who existed in the 13th century and became a popular folk figure in late medieval times. The first recorded ballads about him date from the 14th century. In the folklore, his enemies try to ensnare him by trickery but he survives by using his wits.

Robin Hood is accompanied by a band of followers called his 'Merry Men' and they hide out in Sherwood Forest, in Nottinghamshire. The Merry Men include Little John and, in later versions, monk Friar Tuck and Robin's true love Maid Marian. Robin Hood lives outside the law as a bandit dressed in Lincoln green, who hunts in the forest despite this practice being illegal to all but the nobility.

A detail of the Robin Hood statue at Nottingham Castle, the major historical landmark in Nottingham.

Vintage colour illustration showing Robin Hood and his Merry Men practising with their longbows.

His principal enemy is the rich and corrupt Sheriff of Nottingham. He also opposes King John, who is regarded as having usurped the throne from the rightful monarch Richard the Lionheart, who is away fighting in the Holy Land along with the other Crusaders.

According to the legend, as a child Robin has been cheated out of his birthright by noblemen and has vowed from then on to free the poor from their servitude and redistribute wealth more fairly. His attacks on the wealthy bring him to the attention of the Sheriff of Nottingham, who tries to capture him. However, Robin's loyal band of men are usually able to protect him. In one attempt to snare Robin, the Sheriff holds an archery competition to find and reward the best archer in Nottingham, believing he is sure to enter. Robin Hood does enter the competition but in disguise and wins. The Sheriff realizes his identity too late. He orders his men to arrest him, but by then Robin has escaped back into the forest.

Leprechauns
Ireland

Leprechauns are fairy or sprite figures in Irish folklore, usually depicted as little bearded men wearing a green jacket and hat. They are renowned for being mischievous, quick-witted and difficult to capture. The leprechaun is an iconic symbol of St Patrick's Day, celebrating the patron saint of Ireland. The earliest known reference to leprechauns is in a medieval tale called *Adventure of Fergus son of Leti*.

In Irish folklore, leprechauns are solitary creatures that live underground where they make and mend shoes. They love music and dancing and will often stay up all night enjoying themselves. This probably explains the constant need for new shoes.

If captured by humans, leprechauns will do anything to escape from their captors, even granting them three wishes in exchange for their freedom – but they make sure they get the upper hand. For example, when one captor's wish was to be made ruler of a tropical island, his wish was granted but he found himself ruling an uninhabited island.

Soldiers would often bury their valuables before going to war, and leprechauns would dig them up and claim them for their own. They have amassed a great deal of wealth as a result; they hide their pots of gold at the end of a rainbow, where they can never be found.

An illustration of Fergus, son of Leti. Medieval stories of this mythical king of Ulster contain the first reference to the mischievous leprechauns.

An illustration of a leprechaun.

TRICKSTERS

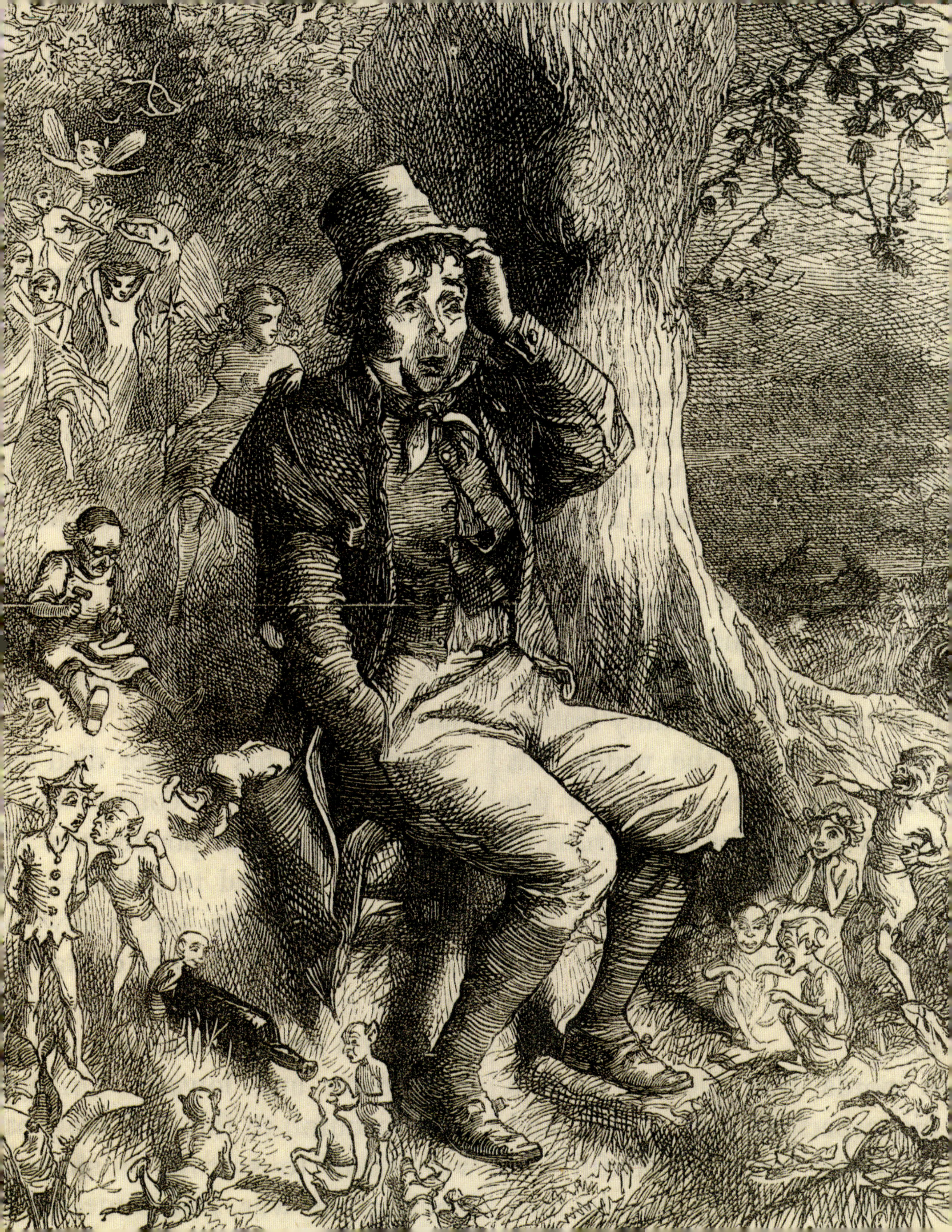

Kitsune

Japan

Kitsune is the Japanese word for fox. The Kitsune are part of the Yokai group of supernatural beings in Japanese folklore. Kitsune possess great intelligence and magical powers. They live for a very long time, and when they reach 100 years old, they are able to change form, or shape-shift into human beings. Kitsune often become beautiful women. Any woman seen alone, particularly at dawn or dusk, could be a Kitsune in disguise.

Every thousand years a Kitsune grows a new tail. Kitsune can have up to nine tails, depending on their age, wisdom and power. A Kitsune's fur becomes gold or white when it gains its ninth tail. The only way to kill one is to chop off all its tails.

There are two main types of Kitsune: the zenko or myobu (literally 'celestial fox'), which is associated with the god Inari (god of rice), and the yako or nogitsune ('field fox' or 'wild fox'), which can be mischievous and even malicious.

Kitsune use their magical powers to play tricks on humans, particularly the overly proud samurai. Kitsune breathe fire and generate fire from their tails and use this fire to lead travellers astray. Kitsune also appear in people's dreams and create optical illusions, which they use to lure humans into their traps. Trickery is usually reserved for men, however, whereas women are possessed.

A 19th-century Kitsune mask from Japan.

A Nekomata or cat demon plays the shamisen next to a Kitsune or fox spirit. From the Bakemono Zukushi Monster Scroll, Edo Period (1603–1868).

Major Yasumichi and the Kitsune

Major Yasumichi lives in a big mansion with extensive grounds. He is tired of the Kitsune running around on his land and causing mischief, so he orders a fox hunt the next day to kill the Kitsune with bows and arrows. The night before the hunt, an old man appears to Major Yasumichi in a dream and respectfully explains that he has lived there for many generations with his family. He apologizes for the trouble his many children and grandchildren cause, and promises to control them and respect Yasumichi in future. When Yasumichi awakes from his dream, he sees a hairless old fox sitting in the same place under the tangerine tree where the old man had appeared in his dream. He cancels the foxhunt and the Kitsune cause no more trouble.

Ivan the Fool
Russia

Ivan the lucky fool is a stock character of Russian folklore. The kind-hearted but simple youngest son of a farmer, he thinks with his heart and not his mind. He lives his life on a sound moral basis, however. His older brothers are smarter and more successful than Ivan, but often unkind and unlucky. Leo Tolstoy published the fairy tale of Ivan the Fool as a short story in 1886, 'Ivan the Fool and his Two Brothers'.

Ivan has two older brothers, Simeon, a soldier, and Taras, a merchant, plus a mute sister, Milania. Their father is a wealthy farmer. Ivan, who works on the farm with his father, isn't very bright. Simeon and Taras are both married and spend all their money on their greedy wives so they go to their father and ask for a share of Ivan's land. Ivan agrees; he is happy to share with his brothers. The Devil is displeased with all this brotherly love and harmony, and wants to cause trouble so sends his imps to put curses on all three brothers. The elder two are already corrupted by their greed and vanity, but Ivan doesn't give in to the imp's tricks. Because of his simple, kind-hearted nature, he captures one of the imps, who then has to grant Ivan's wish. Ivan wishes to be taught magic, and using his new power is able to restore Simeon to his previous status in the army and provide Taras with abundant wealth.

A monument to Ivan the Fool in Tobolsk, Russia.

TRICKSTERS

Ivan the Fool and the firebird. The character of Ivan appears in various incarnations in Russian folk stories. In one tale, Ivan, the youngest of the Tsar's three sons, is sent to patrol the garden to discover who is stealing the Tsar's golden apples. He plucks one of the bird's feathers to show his father.

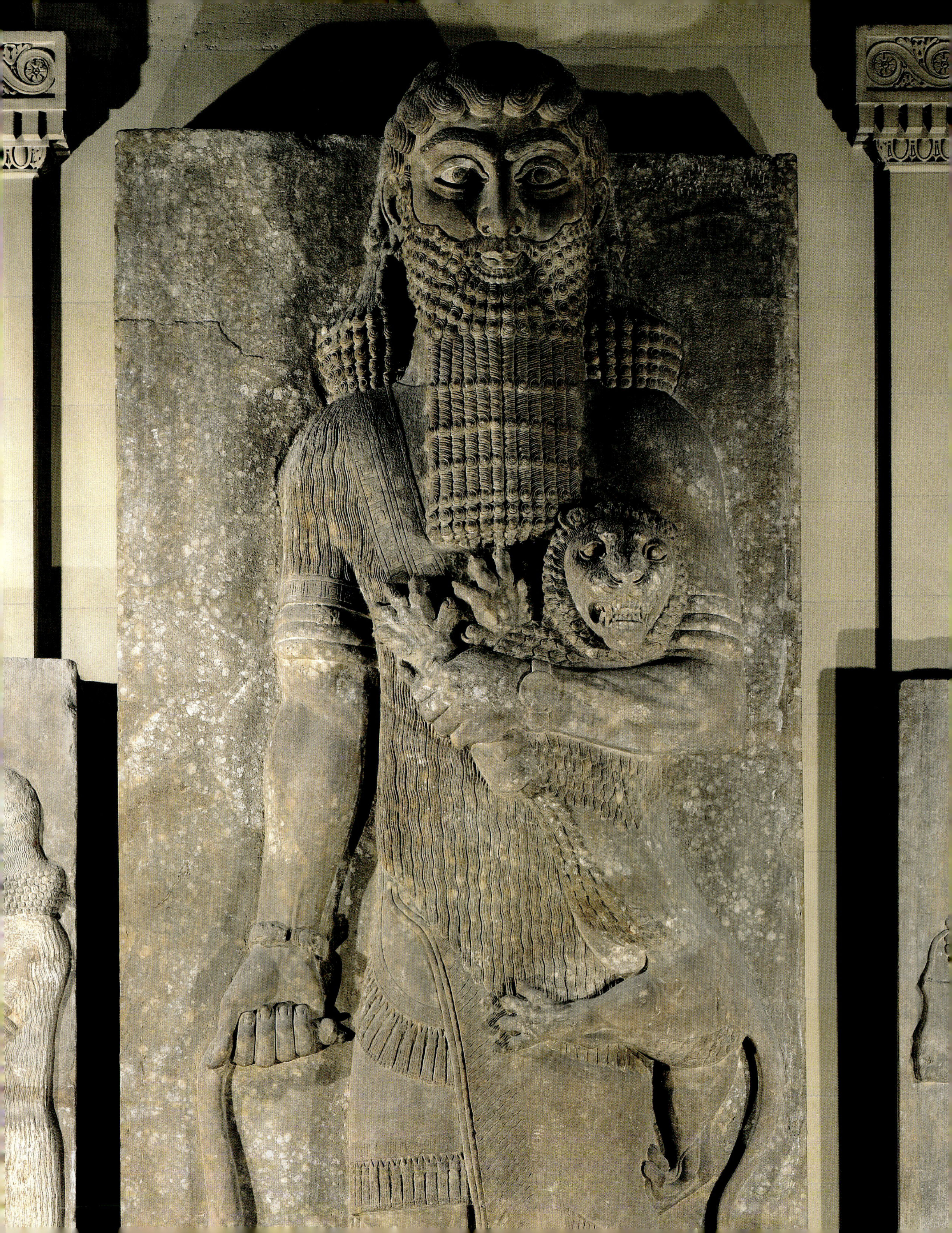

Mythological epics

An epic is a long narrative poem written in a literary style that draws attention to the craft of storytelling and the conventions of narrative. It usually employs an elevated style of language – often declamatory: dramatic, ornate and with sometimes overblown rhetoric. It usually includes heroes of historical or legendary status performing deeds of note. The setting is often worldwide in scope, covering great nations or the entire universe, and the story sometimes veers away from realism to include the supernatural. The action of the epic is of great importance to the people of a nation, and generally those epics are perennial.

Beowulf
Scandinavia

Beowulf, written by an unknown poet, is the longest and greatest surviving Anglo-Saxon poem, believed to have been written between 700 and 1000.

It has 3182 lines of alliterative verse, and is written in a West Saxon dialect of Old English. This epic poem tells of the hero Beowulf and his battles, from youth to old age. The poem is set in sixth-century Denmark.

In Danish mythology, every 500 years or so, a Hag gives birth to a horrible monster called a Grendel. The Grendel has great strength and speed and is immune to human weapons. They are roughly human in shape, stand over 3m (10ft) tall and are covered in fur. Born of a human mother, Grendel is a descendant of the biblical figure Cain, who murdered his brother.

Hrothgar is King of the Danes and lives in the great hall of Heorot. The King is prosperous and shares his wealth and fortune with his men. They live a celebratory life of feasting, drinking and music. When Grendel hears those celebrations from his lair, his envy of their prosperity and bitterness that he has been excluded drives him to attack Heorot. While the King and his men are sleeping, Grendel attacks the hall and kills some of the King's men.

He goes back each night for twelve years, killing more men and causing more chaos. A young warrior called Beowulf from Geatland hears of Hrothgar's troubles and sails to Heorot to help. Grendel is immune to human weaponry, so Beowulf

Beowulf shears off the head of Grendel. Illustration for Hero-Myths and Legends of the British Race *by M. I. Ebbutt (1916).*

MYTHOLOGICAL EPICS

fights him with his bare hands. After a violent struggle, Beowulf manages to tear Grendel's arm from his shoulder. Grendel runs back to his home in the marshes where he dies.

The next day everyone flocks to the hall to hear the news. Everyone is overjoyed and Hrothgar bestows Beowulf with gifts to show his gratitude.

However, Grendel's mother – who has seen the monster die a slow and painful death – vows to avenge her son. The following night, she goes to Heorot and kills one of Hrothgar's men.

When Beowulf hears about this the next day, he searches for the she-devil and eventually finds her near the bottom of the marsh bed, where she lures him into her lair and shows him Grendel's dead body. After a long and difficult battle, Beowulf defeats her and rises to the surface of the water, bringing Grendel's head with him as a trophy.

Everyone in Heorot is overjoyed once more, and Hrothgar showers Beowulf with yet more gifts. When Beowulf leaves, Hrothgar is devastated and weeps. Beowulf returns to his own land a hero, and fifty years on becomes the king of his people, the Geats.

One day, a slave finds a sleeping dragon guarding a pile of treasure, and decides to steal a golden cup. When the dragon awakes and discovers the theft, it attacks the people. Beowulf – now about 70 years old – meets the dragon in battle. Beowulf manages to kill the dragon, but not before the dragon sinks his venomous teeth into Beowulf's neck.

Beowulf briefly finds solace in the fact that he has won the dragon's vast pile of treasure for his people, but then dies from the wound. The Geats are distraught and build memorials for their beloved king. The epic poem closes with a tribute to Beowulf's bravery, kindness and generosity.

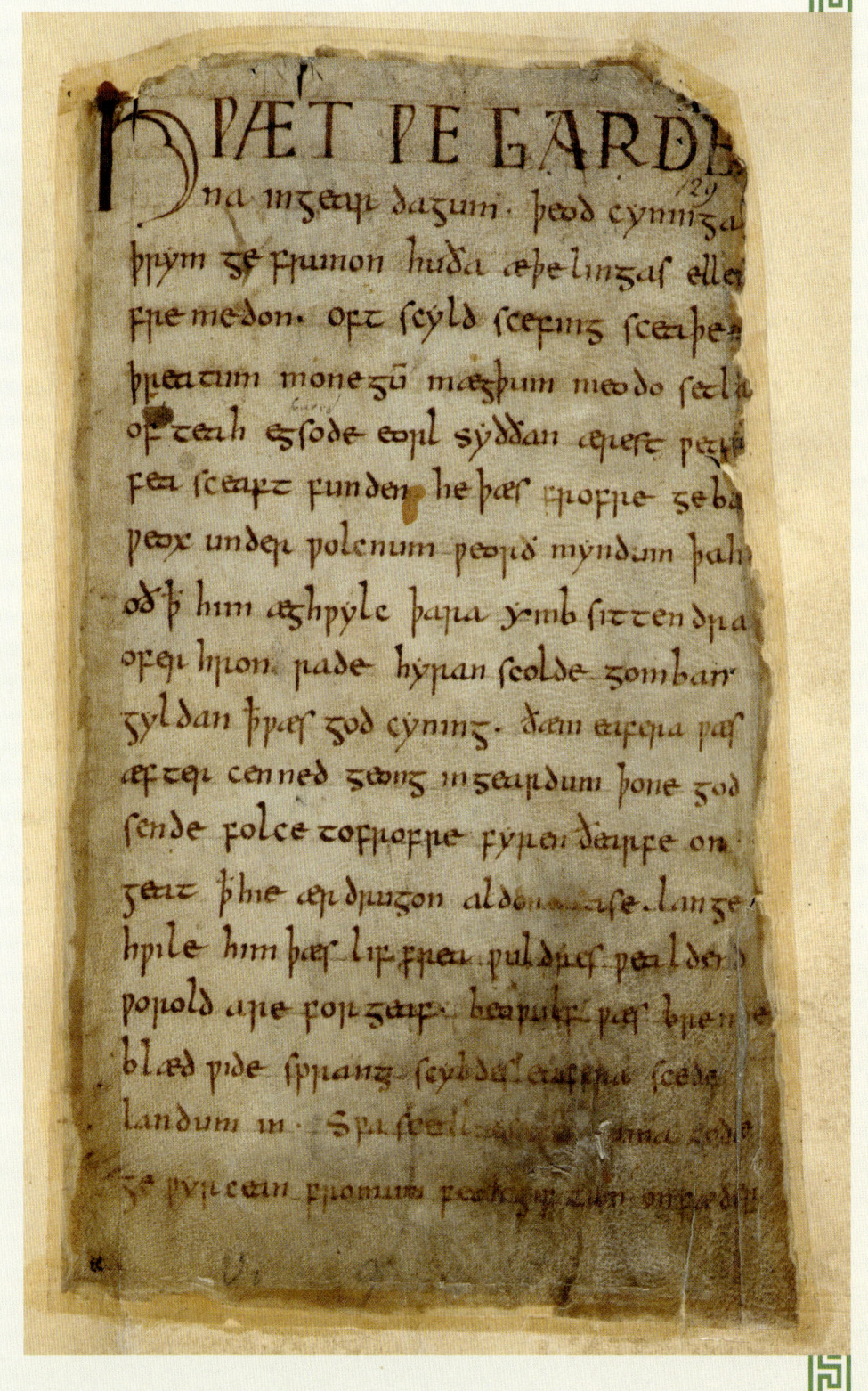

A page from the famous Beowulf, written by an unknown poet between 700 and 1000.

The Iliad and the Odyssey
Greece

The writings of Homer mark the beginning of Greek literature. His authorship of the magnificent epic poems the *Iliad* and the *Odyssey* have made him one of the most influential writers in world history. They are two of the most widely read and celebrated poems of all time, blending elements of Greek history, mythology and culture. They are the first true literary texts we have and the main source of all we know about Greek mythology today.

A pencil drawing on paper of Homer.

Yet little is known of Homer, other than that he was said to be blind. He may even not have been one person but an amalgam of several writers. Homer's world was Greece in the 8th century BC. During his lifetime there was a shift from an oral tradition to the emergence of a Greek alphabet and the practice of story-writing. That century was also marked by an explosion of ideas, including the emergence of the *polis*, the Greek city-state with population centres; the rule of law and civic infrastructure. Homer effectively invented Western civilization, and made real our understanding of ancient history: before him there were only archaeological ruins to record the history of a nation.

Homer's two epic poems reflect a fusion of elements from different ages in the service of a monumental and triumphant history of the Greek empire. He provides a template of cultural values and preserved memories. His works relate to a time long before he was born and of which he knew nothing other than through the stories passed on through an oral tradition.

The Iliad contains the story of the siege of Troy, the actions of Agamemnon and Achilles and Paris' kidnapping of Helen (see also pages 86-7).

The Odyssey continues after the fall of Troy, with the struggle of the hero Odysseus. Both of Homer's epic poems describe human traits and emotions in detail, including vanity, lust, pride and dishonour.

The Fall of Troy and the Escape of Aeneas, *an engraving by Giorgio Ghisi (1520–82).*

The Iliad and the Odyssey

Gilgamesh
Mesopotamia

The *Epic of Gilgamesh* is a Sumerian or Babylonian poem, written between 2150 and 1400BC. King Gilgamesh, the main character in the poem, is the semi-mythical king of Uruk in ancient Mesopotamia. Gilgamesh, one-third human and two-thirds god, rules the kingdom of Uruk and lives in a grand palace, grander than anywhere else in Mesopotamia. He builds huge walls around Uruk to protect his kingdom.

The hero Gilgamesh holding a lion that he has captured; a stone relief from the Palace of Sargon II at Khorsabad (Iraq), c.727.

Gilgamesh holds great power over his people and treats them badly, so they appeal to the sky god, Anu, for help. In response, Anu creates the wild man, Enkidu, to plague Gilgamesh's city. Enkidu attacks the shepherd's livestock, leaving the people without food. The people plead with Gilgamesh to intervene and he sends a temple prostitute, Shamhat, to seduce Enkidu, believing this will tame the wild man.

Enkidu, now tamed, and Shamhat visit the king's palace to find Gilgamesh attending a wedding. Gilgamesh declares that, as king, he has the right to sleep with the bride first. Enkidu is angry at this and challenges Gilgamesh to a fight. If Enkidu wins, Gilgamesh will have to give up his right to have sex with the bride. Gilgamesh wins the fight but honours Enkidu's wishes anyway and they return to the palace as friends.

A few years pass and they become best friends. They leave Uruk together seeking adventure. They venture into the cedar forest to try to kill the giant Humbaba. Gilgamesh and Enkidu are victorious, but after returning to Uruk, Enkidu falls ill and dies.

After Enkidu's death, Gilgamesh wishes to know the secret of immortality. He hears that an ancient man holds the secret and so he leaves Uruk and sets off to find the man. After a long journey, Gilgamesh reaches the Sea of Death, which will carry him to the ancient man. However, two stone monsters bar his way. Gilgamesh kills them both and scatters their stony parts all around. An old man appears and introduces himself as the boatman who will transport Gilgamesh. He says Gilgamesh has made a terrible mistake in killing the two stone giants because they are the only things that can come into contact with the Sea of Death without disintegrating.

The boatman instructs Gilgamesh to chop down three hundred trees and make a hundred oars, as each one will dissolve on contact with the water. When the oars are ready, they set off on their journey. They travel to an island where they see a single house in which the ancient man lives.

The ancient man says he will give Gilgamesh eternal life if he can complete a challenge: to stay awake for six days and seven nights. Gilgamesh agrees, but soon falls asleep. When he wakes up, he tries to deny being asleep, but the old man shows him six loaves of bread that his wife has baked – one for each day the king has been asleep.

So Gilgamesh loses the opportunity to achieve immortality. The ancient man then tells him that there is a plant at the bottom of the ocean that can restore his youth. Gilgamesh reaches it by tying rocks to his feet so he can walk into the ocean. When he resurfaces with the plant, he is so exhausted that he falls asleep on the beach. A snake comes along and eats the plant, sheds its skin and becomes young again. When Gilgamesh wakes up, he sees the snake reborn and realizes his hopes are lost.

He returns to Uruk and, on seeing his great palace again, understands that man isn't supposed to have everlasting life, but instead should leave behind a legacy to be enjoyed by others.

The partially broken tablet V of the Epic of Gilgamesh *from Mesopotamia, Iraq. The tablet dates back to the old Babylonian period, 2003–1595BC.*

Tuatha dé Danann
Ireland

In Irish-Celtic mythology, the Tuatha de Danann are a race of Irish gods, founded by the goddess Danu (the term literally means 'people of the goddess Danu'). Danu's son, Dagda is the most powerful leader of the Dananns.

The epic of the Tuatha dé Danann is the first cycle of Irish storytelling. The stories of these mythical Irish fairy folk and gods are detailed in the 12th-century *Book of Invasions*.

The Tuatha dé Danann come from four mythical cities, Falias, Gorias, Finius and Murias, and have received four magical treasures or talismans, one from each city. These magical talismans are Dagda's Cauldron, the Spear of Lugh, the Stone of Fal and the Sword of Nuad. Some say they arrived by boat, and others suggest they floated in on clouds. Little else is known about the Tuatha de Danann prior to their arrival in Ireland, other than that they have perfected the art of magic.

A mural of a queen of the Tuatha dé Danann slain at the battle of Tailtiu Béal Feirste, Ardoyne, Belfast.

Following their arrival in Ireland, the Tuatha dé Danann fight three battles, beginning with the First Battle of Magh Tuiredh, in which they defeat the indigenous population, the Firbolgs. Next comes the Second Battle of Magh Tuiredh, in which they defeat a race of sea monsters called the Fomorians.

In the third battle, the Tuatha dé Danann are defeated by the Milesians from Spain, led by King Milesius, and banished to the underworld. Their homes in the underworld are called Sidhe, and the Tuatha dé Danann are also known as Aes Sidhe ('people of the sidhe'). They occasionally return to aid mortals in their wars, always on the side of justice and righteousness. The gods have now evolved from Celtic deities into fairy people.

Dagda is one of the most important gods and the most powerful leader of the Dananns. He is still celebrated in Ireland today. In this image, two Dagda followers are preparing for the St Patrick's Parade in Dublin.

Hallowe'en

Hallowe'en derives from the ancient Celtic festival of Samhain ('summer's end') when the fairy folk (as the Tuatha become) walk abroad for one evening. Anyone who encounters one of the fairy folk at this time risks being kidnapped and taken back with them to their underground dwellings, so it is important to appease them with gifts. Now children dress up as witches and demons on Hallowe'en and threaten householders with spells ('tricks') unless given treats to make them go away.

Tuatha dé Danann

Mabinogion
Britain

The *Mabinogion* texts are a collection of medieval Welsh stories and represent a golden age of narrative prose in Wales. They concern the mythological past and heroic age of the British Isles. The collection has been widely influential, giving rise to timeless literary figures such as Merlin and Arthur.

One of the twelve tales of the Mabinogion, *the collection of Welsh myths.*

Scholars differ as to the meaning of the word *Mabinogion*: some think it the plural of the Welsh word *mabinogi*, which means youthful career. Others think its derivation is from the Welsh word *mabinog*, meaning an aspirant to bardic honour. The stories in the *Mabinogion* are compiled from texts found in two manuscripts, the *White Book of Rhydderch* (c.1300-25) and the *Red Book of Hergest* (c.1375-1425).

There are eleven separate tales in this collection. The first four tales, called collectively 'The Four Branches of the Mabinogi', are divided into Pwyll, Branwen, Manawydan, and Math. Their connecting link, now obscure, is the story of Prince Gwri (later called Pryderi). Themes include loyalty, love, marriage, fidelity and incest. The setting is a mythical landscape that contains magical horses and giants.

One of the tales, the 'Story of Kilhwch and Olwen', composed before 1100, is an early example of an Arthurian tale. 'The Dream of Rhonabwy', written before 1175, contains Welsh traditions about King Arthur. There is a story based on the legend of Emperor Maximus, 'The Dream of Maxim Wledig'. The last group in the *Mabinogion* consists of three Arthurian romances, 'Geraint', 'The Lady of the Fountain' and 'Peredur'. It is probable that the first two shared common sources written in French, and that the last drew on the vast body of Grail tradition. Others, 'The Four Branches', 'Kilhwch' and the romances are invaluable in the study of the Arthurian legend.

The texts first came to general literary prominence in the mid 19th century, when Lady Charlotte Guest translated the collection and published it under the title *The Mabinogion*, using the *Red Book of Hergest* as her source. Later, the *White Book of Rhydderch* was discovered, containing older, finer versions of the tales in Guest's work. In 1929, T.P. Ellis and J. Lloyd published a translation based on a composite of the tales in both the Red and White books.

The spelling in these works varies widely depending on their source.

Tales of the Mabinogion; carved wooden sculpture at Cwmcarn Forest Drive in the South Wales Valleys.

THE POPUL VUH
MESOAMERICA

The *Popol Vuh* is the story of creation according to the Quiche Maya (also spelled K'iche Maya), the people of the region now known as Guatemala. According to the *Popol Vuh*, humans have been created in order to praise their creator. Among the central characters of the *Popol Vuh* are the Hero Twins Hunahpu and Ixbalanque, who slay monsters and descend into the underworld where they defeat the rulers there and later become the sun and the moon.

The world has been created using maize, a staple in Mesoamerican culture (but used here as an agricultural metaphor). The first humans are defective, however, so the creator Hurricane destroys everything with a flood. After this, an imposter named Seven Macaw tries to take over as the principal deity but is defeated by the Hero Twins. The *Popol Vuh* describes how the god-magicians Gucumatz and Tepeu try to make humans from mud and clay after the flood, but are then forced to use maize again.

The story spans the time from creation until the Spanish conquest in the 16th century. On 12 July 1562, the Spanish Bishop Diego de Landa burned as many Mayan books as he could find but he didn't have jurisdiction in the Quiche region, so the *Popol Vuh* survived. It is estimated that the *Popol Vuh* was written between 1554 and 1558 – a time when the beliefs and traditions of the Mayan culture would not have been tolerated by the Christian conquerors. The author is unknown but it is likely that the work is based on earlier texts or an oral tradition.

Originally it was a single, long poem but was divided into four parts when it was translated into European languages.

Book 1: Out of nothing the gods create all the world and all living things except humans. They try to create humans, too, so that there is someone to worship them, but fail as the humans they make are heartless and don't remember their creators. The gods destroy everything with a great flood and are then left alone to glorify themselves.

Book 2: The deity Seven Macaw thinks too highly of himself and so the Hero Twins, Hunahpu and Ixbalanque, set out to destroy

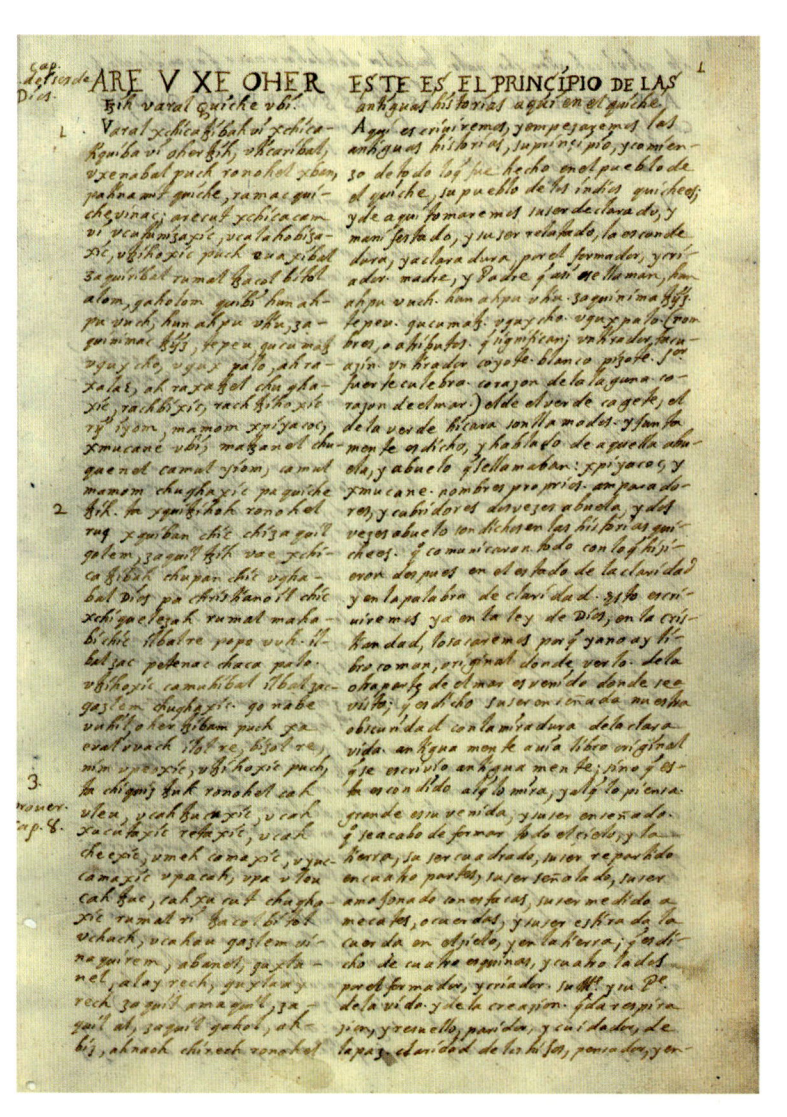

The oldest surviving written account of the Popol Vuh, *from 1701.*

him. Seven Macaws refuses to acknowledge the work of the other gods and, when the Hero Twins kill him and his sons, balance is restored.

Book 3: We learn about the history and the family of the Hero Twins. After many adventures on earth, they descend to the underworld to take over there, beating the Lords of Death in a ball game. Eventually they ascend the World Tree into the sky where they become the sun and the moon.

Book 4: Humans are re-created from maize, this time successfully. The gods give the men wives and teach them to grow food, and they are content. The book concludes with the story of the migration of the Quiche and their genealogy.

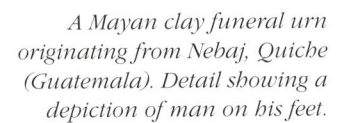

A Mayan clay funeral urn originating from Nebaj, Quiche (Guatemala). Detail showing a depiction of man on his feet.

Corn fields on a mountain under blue sky in Baja Verapaz, Guatemala. In the Popul Vuh, *the beginning of the world is described in terms of farming, and maize is used as a fundamental material for creation.*

The Popul Vuh

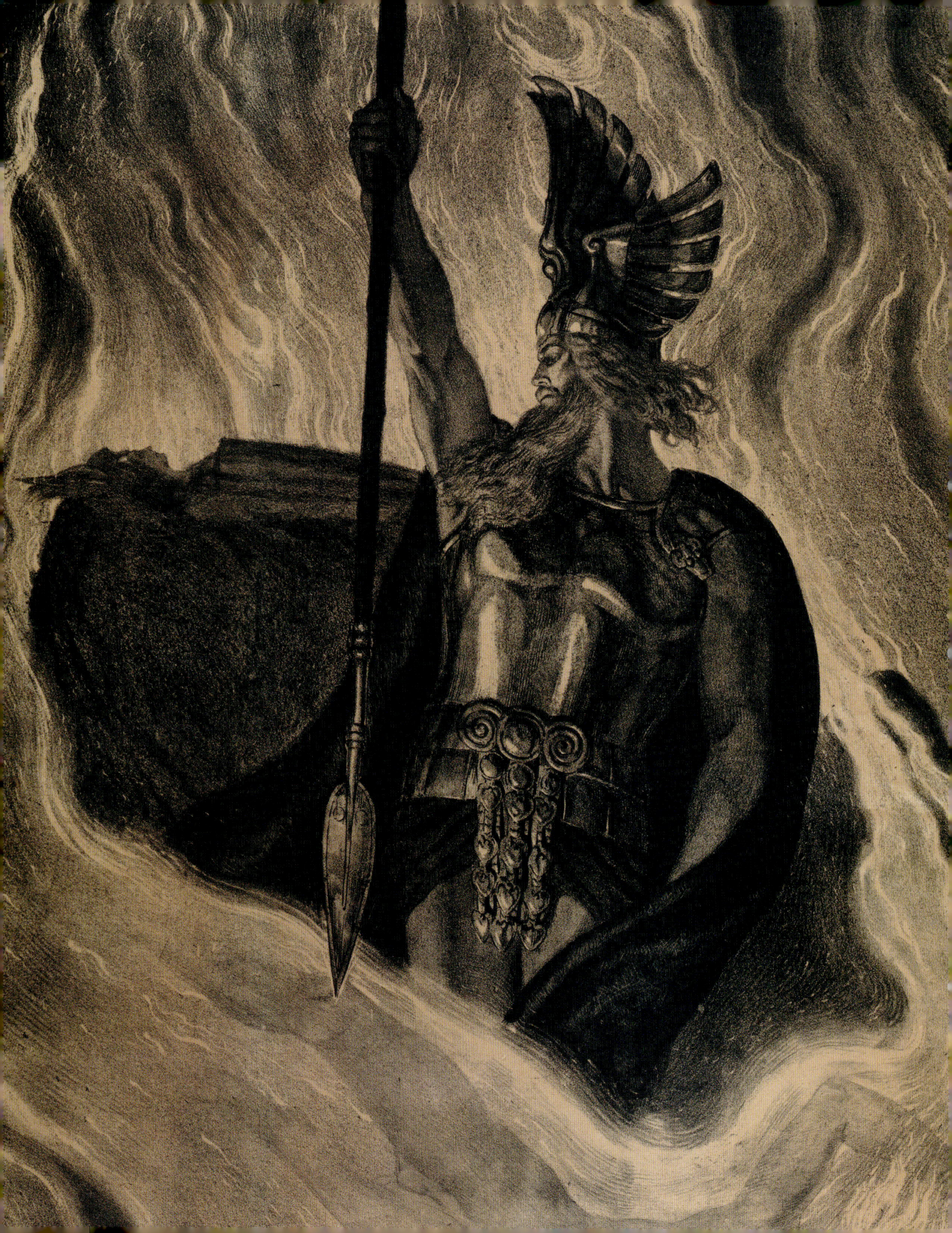

Death and the Afterlife

There are elaborate scenes of death in the world of myth. Such tales also contain complex ideas of what might be expected after death has occurred. It is understandable that the suddenness and finality of death demands the creation of detailed psychological and philosophical frameworks in order to make sense of it – and this is where notions of an 'afterlife' take root. It is true that every religion seeks to provide a narrative of what happens to us once we leave this world. Some of these myths can be profoundly enduring as, even today, we are still no closer to having concrete answers to the universal phenomenon of death and consciousness.

Heaven and hell
World mythologies

At the heart of all world mythologies lies a belief in a supernatural realm beyond our earthbound experience. In most mythologies, the universe is divided into three tiers: the realm of the gods (often called heaven), the earth (where humans live) and an underworld (often referred to as hell).

In many early traditions, such as Greek and Mesopotamian, those levels are born from Chaos, the universe in its primordial state, and fashioned by the gods themselves. In Christianity, the essential characteristic of heaven, hell or purgatory is that they are stages in being a spirit (angel or demon) rather than actual places. Metaphorically, heaven is the dwelling place of God and when people who have welcomed God into their lives die, they will join him and enjoy the fullness of communion with God.

Those believers are loved in a special way by the Father, and have been raised with Christ to be made citizens of Heaven, populated by angels. Christians look forward to heaven as a place where they will find complete healing, and where sadness and pain are banished forever. The Christian faith has no belief in reincarnation.

If man rejects God, he separates himself from joyful communion with Him and goes to hell when he dies.

Hell is the ultimate consequence of sin itself – not a punishment imposed by God, but self-imposed due to lack of faith. Hell is a state of eternal damnation, usually portrayed as a burning pit of fire, that is populated by devils. In the Bible, Jesus compares hell with Gehenna, which was a rubbish dump outside Jerusalem. Satan appears first as an angel in heaven, but is cast down into hell after rebelling against God. Satan then becomes the ultimate source of evil and temptation, and the head of a hierarchy of demons. In the three days that follow the crucifixion, Christ descends into hell to save the souls of the dead.

For those who are neither saint nor sinner but somewhere in between (open to God but still imperfectly), their journey to heaven requires some purification known as 'purgatory'. Those destined for God must be perfect, so those who do not yet possess this integrity must be purified. Again, purgatory is not so much a place as a condition of existence.

Ancient Greek mythology features two underworlds: Hades, ruled over by the god of the same name, and Tartarus, which lies beneath it. Tartarus is similar to the Christian idea of hell.

Allegory of Heaven and Hell *by Spanish artist Claudio Coello (1642–93).*

DEATH AND THE AFTERLIFE

The right-hand panel depicting hell from the Triptych of Earthly Vanity and Divine Salvation *by Hans Hemling, c.1485.*

VALHALLA
SCANDINAVIA

Our understanding of Norse mythology, including Valhalla, has come almost entirely from one work, the 13th-century *Prose Edda*, compiled by the Icelandic historian, politician and poet Snorri Sturluson and based on stories circulated in the oral tradition.

A detail of the legend of Valhalla from the island of Gotland, 9th century.

Odin Calling Up the Fire, *by Franz Stassen, c.1914.*

In Norse mythology, Valhalla is an enormous hall located in Asgard, the realm of the Aesir gods and also the bravest and fiercest of Norse warriors. It is ruled over by Odin, who decides which warriors who have died in combat will travel there after death, led by the Valkyries. The warriors will be cremated with their weapons and worldly possessions, so they will be reunited with these goods on arrival at Valhalla. Warriors who are not so honoured go to goddess Freyja's field, Folkvangr, instead.

The fallen warriors of Valhalla are called Einherjar. They are not chosen for their moral virtues, but for their strength and bravery. Reaching Valhalla is regarded as the greatest achievement for a warrior, because it means the new arrival has been the victor of many battles and has died a heroic death. The Vikings therefore sought out worthy opponents in order to improve their chances of being one of the chosen.

Although Valhalla is the realm of the gods, it isn't their only one. The Aesir occupy all of Asgard, and the other group of gods – the Vanir – occupy Vanaheimr. The hall is majestic and the ceiling is thatched with golden shields; the framework made from spears. It is guarded by wolves and eagles.

Those chosen to live in Valhalla are there to help Odin prepare for Ragnarök and join the fight against the giant wolf, Fenrir (see page 146-7). Therefore a defining feature of Valhalla is the constant military training and preparation for battle.

Valhalla 189

Orpheus and Eurydice
Greece

The ancient legend of Orpheus and Eurydice concerns the fateful love of Orpheus for the beautiful Eurydice, an oak Nymph and possibly also the daughter of Apollo. Orpheus, son of Oeager (or Apollo) and the muse Calliope, is a Thracian who lives in a region bordering Olympus. He is a singer, musician and poet who plays the lyre. He has also invented the cithara, a seven-stringed lyre.

Orpheus and Eurydice are married. One day she is walking along a river, pursued by an admirer, when she steps on a snake that bites her and she dies.

Orpheus is inconsolable and travels to the underworld to bring her back. When he arrives, he uses his singing to charm the monsters who guard the underworld. As Orpheus has gone to such lengths to prove his love, Hades, the god of the underworld, agrees to return Eurydice to him, but there is a condition. Orpheus must return to earth with his wife following behind; he is told not to look back at her before they leave the underworld or he will lose her.

Orpheus has nearly reached daylight when doubt seizes him. He isn't certain that Eurydice is really behind him, so he turns round to check. As a result Eurydice dies a second time and this time Orpheus cannot rescue her. Entry to the underworld is now barred to him forever, and he returns to the human world devastated.

After this, Orpheus spurns involvement with women and surrounds himself with young men, one of whom, Calais, becomes his

An engraving by the Italian artist Agostino Carracci depicting Orpheus trying to pull his love free from the flames of Hades.

An ancient statue of Orpheus with a lyre in his left hand.

lover. Orpheus is murdered by women for 'inventing' homosexuality, and his body is chopped into pieces. After his murder, a plague spreads through Thrace and an oracle says that the people will have to seek out Orpheus's severed head. They find it at the mouth of the Meles river, bloody and still singing.

Orpheus' head became an oracle, a link with the supernatural realm consulted by mortals. Orpheus' soul is taken to the Elysian Fields where, dressed in white, it continues to sing for the benefit of the Blessed Ones.

Izanagi in the underworld
Japan

In Japanese mythology, earth in its early stages resembled oil floating on water. From those murky waters, a reed sprouts up and a divine couple are born. Several more are born in this way and the eighth couple are Izanagi ('He who invites') and Izanami ('She who invites'), who are entrusted with creating the earth.

Izanagi dips his spear into the water and stirs; when he lifts his spear from the water, the droplets that fall create an island. The two deities descend to the island. After a rocky start to the marriage, because Izanami spoke first at the wedding ceremony (see page 22), she gives birth to many children. These became the eight main islands of Japan, six minor islands, and several deities to inhabit those islands.

When Izanami gives birth to the fire god Kagutsuchi, the terrible burns she suffers cause her death. Izanagi's tears over his wife's death create another deity. Izanagi then beheads the fire deity who has caused his wife's death. Izanagi misses her terribly and decides to journey to the underworld, Yomi-no-kuni, to bring her back.

In the darkness of the underworld, Izanagi calls out to Izanami to return with him to the land of the living. She replies that it is already too late as she has tasted the food of hell. However, she will talk to the gods of the underworld to see if she can leave, and she asks Izanagi to do one thing: not to look at her until she returns.

A hanging scroll depicting God Izanagi and Goddess Izanami from 18th-century Japan.

Izanagi, however, becomes impatient and goes looking for her; when he finds his once-beautiful wife, he sees that she is a rotting corpse. Ashamed to be seen in this condition, Izanami chases Izanagi out of the underworld and sends the eight deities of thunder, born from her body, to pursue him.

Izanagi escapes the underworld but, feeling sullied by this contact with the world of the dead, goes to the island of Tsukiji to purify himself in the river.

As he strips off his clothes, more deities are born from them. He finishes the purification process by washing his left eye (giving birth to the goddess of the sun, Amaterasu), his right eye (giving birth to the moon goddess Tsukiyomi) and his nose (giving birth to the god Susanoo).

Izanagi orders Amaterasu to rule the plain of heaven, Tsukiyomi to rule the night, and Susanoo to rule the seas. The first two obey their father, but Susanoo says he wants to descend to the underworld to be with his mother, after saying goodbye to his older sister. He ascends to heaven to say farewell, but then proceeds to cause chaos and darkness, and is eventually driven out. He settles in Suga with his new wife, and does not join Izanami in the underworld.

The two rocks of Meoto Iwa (wedded rocks) connected by a rope, representing the union of the gods Izanami and Izanagi.

THE HEAVENLY CIVIL SERVICE
CHINA

In Chinese mythology, the lives of the gods and goddesses mirror life on earth in many ways. The Chinese emperor has a huge civil service of ministers to help him govern the country, and in heaven the gods and goddesses are organized in a similar way with their own 'governor', the Jade Emperor.

The Heavenly Civil Service, also called the Heavenly Court, is divided into different departments to help the Jade Emperor rule. The gods act as messengers between heaven and earth, and the only human to whom the Jade Emperor himself speaks is the earthly emperor.

The gods in Chinese mythology are bureaucrats with a strict order of rank and clear duties. Every month they write reports, and every year those reports are presented to the Jade Emperor who promotes or demotes gods accordingly, depending on their performance. The earthly paperwork is presented in the same way.

The characteristic unique to unique to Chinese mythology is that the gods are not immutable, the explanation being that most Chinese gods are not divine in origin, but men who have been deified after death.

The gods each have their own dwelling place, and heaven is divided into hierarchies (from nine to thirty-three levels, depending on the version). The gods with the highest seniority in office live on the top level.

The Forbidden City in Beijing, China, was constructed between 1406 and 1420. It was the centre of government and consisted of nearly a thousand separate buildings. Taking into account the complex civic scheme of China's medieval period, it is not hard to see the profound influence of the ancient myth of the Heavenly Civil Service on Chinese culture and politics.

DEATH AND THE AFTERLIFE

The Jade Emperor (also August Personage of Jade or Father-Heaven) is the top-ranking god, who created humans from clay and left them in the sun to dry; it then started to rain and he could not get some of the statues under shelter in time. Those that were damaged in the rain constitute the sick people of the world.

The Jade Emperor lives in a palace identical to the one inhabited by the earthly emperor.

Although recognized as the greatest god, the Jade Emperor is, in fact the second in the supreme triad: the first being the Heavenly Master of the First Origin, who precedes the Jade Emperor, and the third being the Heavenly Master of the Dawn of Jade of the Golden Door, who will one day succeed him.

The Jade Emperor is always portrayed wearing the Chinese-style high-ceremonial costume with dragons embroidered on the garments – just like the clothes worn by the earthly emperor.

The Jade Emperor, ruler of Heaven and all realms of existence below including Man and Hell, according to Daoist mythology.

The Heavenly Civil Service

Tuonela, Land of the Dead
Finland

In Finnish mythology, Tuonela (also Manala) is the Land of the Dead. The idea of the afterworld as a place of punishment is not part of Finnish mythology. Across many world myth systems, and before Christianity, people were not segregated into good and bad after death; all would expect the same fate.

Tuonela is controlled by the death god Tuoni and his queen Tuonetar. According to the Kalevala, a 19th-century work of epic poetry based on Finnish oral folklore and mythology and compiled by Elias Lönnrot, this kingdom of the dead is darker than other lands, although the sun does shine and forests flourish.

Tuonela is located far to the north behind a dangerous black river. Tuoni's maid takes the dead over the river where they became ghosts.

Lemminkäinen, one of the heroes of the Kalevala, tries to capture the black swan of Tuonela, so that he can win the hand of a young woman. He is not successful and drowns in the river of Tuonela, where his body is ripped to shreds by Tuoni's son.

The only person to escape unscathed from an expedition to Tuonela is Väinämöinen, who goes there in search of the charms needed to finish building a boat. He succeeds in crossing the river, but is captured by Tuonetar, who throws a

An artist's impression of the black river of Tuonela and the souls of the dead.

The mother of Lemminkäinen waits by the body of her murdered son, one of the heroes of the Kalevala. At this moment, a bee appears bringing with it a drop of honey from the halls of the god Ukko that will restore the warrior to life.

net across the river to stop him returning. However, by changing his form into a serpent, he manages to slither through Tuonetar's net and escape across the river.

Tuoni and Tuonetar have several daughters who are divinities of suffering, including Kipu-Tytto (goddess of illness) and Loviatar, who couples with the Wind and gives birth to nine monsters. Death is personified by Kalma ('the odour of a corpse') who reigns over the graves. The demon Surma stands on the threshold of Kalma's abode.

Despite those gruesome gods, the afterlife in Tuonela is not very different from life on earth. There is a sun, a moon, forests and animals. Traditionally the Finnish bury their dead with useful items to help them on their journey to, and arrival at, Tuonela, such as weapons, snow-shoes and food.

Tuonela, Land of the Dead

The lingering spirits and ghosts
Africa

The Bantu peoples represent up to 600 ethnic groups living across central and southern Africa who all speak the Bantu language. The phrase 'Bantu mythology', therefore, refers to recurring themes found in most Bantu cultures. The core of Bantu religion and mythology is the cult of the dead. Though different tribes, and even individuals in the same tribe, may hold different beliefs, there is a common theme that death does not end all – a ghost lives on when the body dies and is able to influence the affairs of the living. Therefore the spirits of the departed are recognized and honoured and it is Bantu custom to give offerings to the deceased spirits.

Ghosts can communicate with the living through their dreams, as well as through signs and omens, and mediums or prophets. They can cause disaster to a family or tribe who has abandoned them, bring judgement on undiscovered sins, or help people in need.

The ghosts do not go on forever but last only as long as they are remembered by their family or tribes. Parents and grandparents are always commemorated and sacrifices made to them, but preceding generations maintain a precarious existence, vying for a share in the offerings. This means that, with the exception of important chiefs and heroes, most ghosts disappear after approximately three generations through lack of support.

Some tribes believe in reincarnation and that the life of a ghost continues for as long as there is a child in the family. Therefore the ghost only dies if the family line ends.

In Bantu mythology, there are many stories of people returning from death in the form of chameleons and other reptiles.

The spirits of the dead can be consulted for advice. For example, if a member of the Yao tribe is going on a long journey, he will visit his chief who will drop a handful of flour on the ground, then cover it with a cone or pot. If the flour hasn't moved the next day, that is a good omen and the man will set off on his journey with an easy mind; if, however, the flour has moved, it is seen as an omen from the spirits that he should not undertake the journey.

Another common belief is that the dead can come back in animal form, usually as snakes or lizards, particularly chameleons. The Atonga of Lake Nyasa believe that you can choose which animal you will turn into by taking certain medications before your death.

There is a general belief that ghosts hang around graves or the huts they once lived in before disappearing into the underground country of the dead. This ghost country can be reached through caves or holes in the ground. A popular folk tale tells of people who follow animals, such as porcupines, into their burrows, only to mistakenly end up in the land of the dead. The story is told so often it seems to originate from everywhere the Bantu language is spoken.

If someone is ill or if there is a natural disaster, such as a drought or a flood, it may be due to the anger of the spirits.

An engraving of a Bantu funeral, from 1811.

The lingering spirits and ghosts

The River Styx and the underworld
Greece

In Greek mythology, the River Styx forms the boundary between earth and the underworld (Hades). The Styx encircles Hades and the underworld. Styx means 'hate' or 'detestation'.

The underworld contains different areas in which the dead reside. Elysium is where the souls of good mortals are sent. The Asphodel Meadows is where ordinary mortals are sent to toil. Tartarus is for those mortals who have led sinful lives. The River Styx connects all those places and separates the dead from the living.

An illustration of Charon's boat, by Auguste Feyen-Perrin, published in L'Illustration Journal Universel, *Paris, 1857.*

In classical Greek mythology, Hermes leads the dead to the ferry crossing and Charon (also Kharon) ferries the dead across the Styx in his boat. Therefore the dead are always buried with a coin under their tongue to pay for their crossing. If they do not have the coin (a 'danake' or 'Charon's obul'), they will be left to wander up and down the banks of the River Styx as restless spirits for a hundred years. Some who do not have a coin may try to swim across, but very few will make it.

Cerberus is a monstrous three-headed dog who guards the underworld. The sight of the huge monster is the first that greets the souls of the dead when they arrive. Gods swear binding oaths by the river, but those who do not follow through with their oaths lose their voices for nine years, and are then exiled from the council of the gods for a further nine years.

Psyche's final task from her rival Venus, jealous of her beauty, is to descend to the underworld to collect water from the river Styx.

A bronze statuette of Hermes seated on a rock.

The River Styx and the underworld

Rebirth cycles and the next life
World mythologies

Rebirth, also known as reincarnation, is the philosophical or religious concept of cyclic existence; the belief that after death we will be reborn into a new physical body or form, or the soul will transfer into another living thing. The idea of rebirth first appears in ancient Indian texts dating from around 700BC. Belief in reincarnation is shared by a wide variety of cultures and people, including the ancient Greeks, ancient Egyptians and Australian Aboriginal people. Many mythologies tell of heroes or other characters who die and then come back to life as other people, animals or plants.

Asclepius was a Greek hero and god of medicine and healing. This 19th-century engraving depicts his reincarnation as a snake in Rome in the year 293BC. The cult of Asclepius was prevalent for centuries and was adopted in Roman culture.

Reincarnation is a central tenet in all major Indian religions: Hinduism, Buddhism, Sikhism and Jainism share beliefs in *samsara* (an unending chain) and *karma* (the sum of a person's actions through many lives). In essence, an individual's reincarnation depends on the way they live this life. If they live a good, moral life, they will be reborn into a higher class; if they lead a bad, immoral life, they will be reborn into a lower class or even as an animal.

Hindus believe that seven is a holy number; everything religious is associated with that number. Every human is given seven chances to be reborn in a physical form. They also have seven chances to perform good deeds in this physical form. If they do, they will complete their journey to heaven after completing seven lives. If they do not, they will remain trapped in a cycle of birth, death and rebirth.

Most Aboriginal Australians believe that human souls come from the spirits left behind by ancestral beings while on spiritual walkabout during their Dreamtime. The birth of a child is caused by an ancestral spirit entering a woman's body. The person's spirit is returned to the ancestral powers after death.

According to many African beliefs, the souls of dead people linger by their grave or their previous home, waiting to find another body, human or animal, to

A Chinese painting on silk from 983, depicts the six paths of rebirth and Ksitigarbha, a bodhisattva who vows to take responsibilty for all beings until the coming of the next buddha.

inhabit. Other African traditions state that ancestors are reborn as their own descendants, or as animals associated with their tribe. The Yoruba believed that babies are the reincarnation of their ancestors, and call boys 'Father Has Returned' and girls 'Mother Has Returned'.

In ancient Egypt, a soul could pass through a variety of species, such as mammals, marine life and birds, before becoming human again. This entire cycle could take 3,000 years.

In Norse mythology, ancient kings are regarded as reincarnations of the god Freyr.

A belief in reincarnation was held by several historic figures among ancient Greek philosophers, such as Plato and Socrates.

Reincarnation is not always regarded as a human phenomenon. In the Arctic regions, the Inuit people perform ceremonies for the creatures they kill, so that the animal's spirit can be reborn and hunted again in the future.

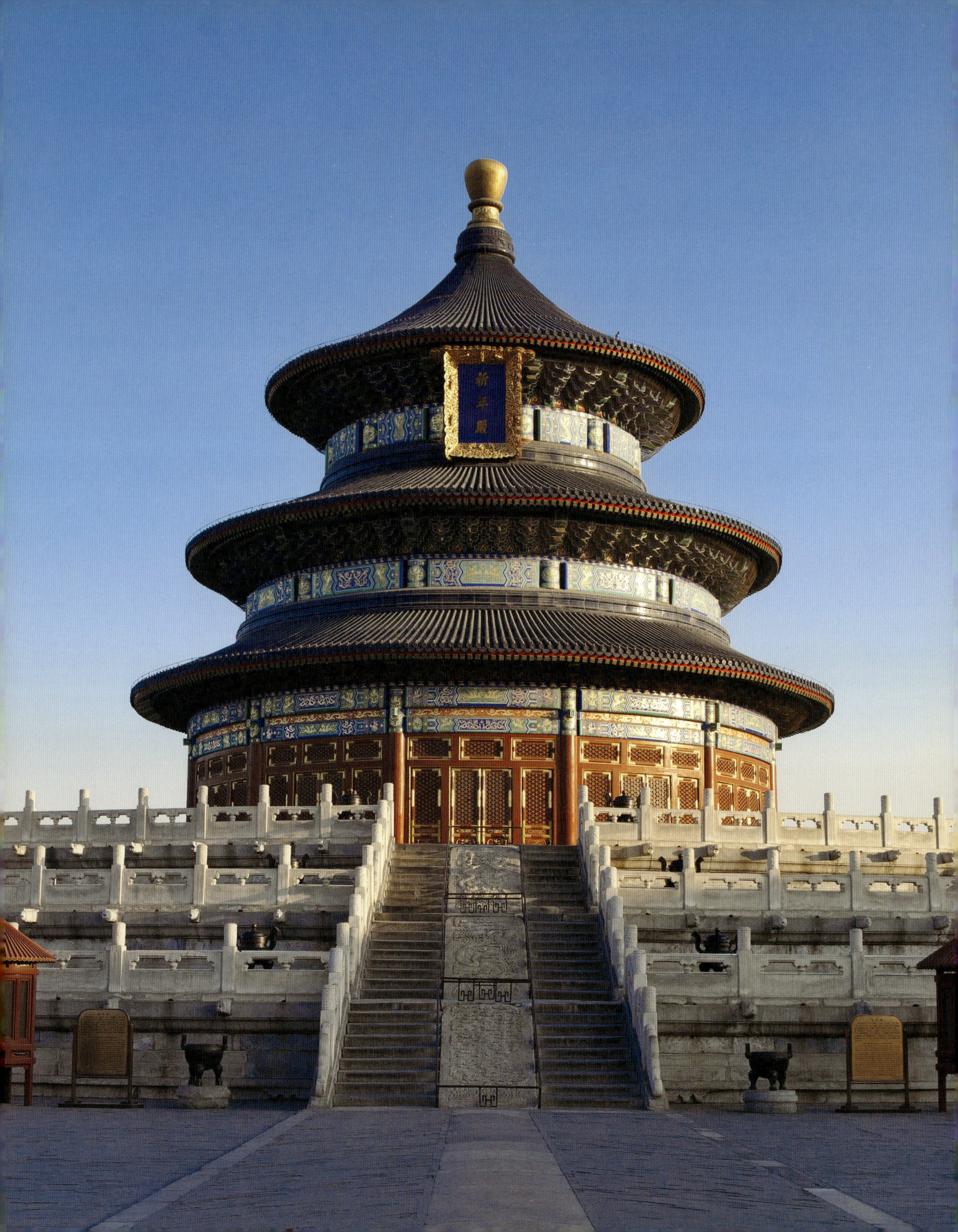

Blurring history, legend and mythology

In a number of myths there are references to evidence from written history or archaeological remains that identify characters, deities and heroes as real-life humans who once lived on the earth. Undoubtedly this ambiguity is the result of generations handing down oral tales alongside scraps of history and thus creating an organic blurring of the real and the imagined.

Manco Cápac: the legendary founder of the Inca dynasty

Peru

Manco Cápac is the son of the sun-god Inti, and founder of the Inca empire. One version of Inca mythology tells how Manco Cápac is sent to earth by his father to build a civilized city and progress the human race. Manco Cápac emerges from the underworld (or Lake Titicaca) with his tapac-yauri, or gold staff, and wanders the Andes and surrounding valleys to find the perfect spot to build a city. He uses his golden staff to test the earth. When he finds a valley where his staff sinks into the earth without resistance he decides this is the spot he seeks. He begins to build his city, which he names Cuzco.

Manco Cápac gathers humans – who at the time are still living wild – to live with him and help him build. He gives them the Quechua language, and teaches them about fire, agriculture, weaving and weapons. He is a ruthless man and soon begins planning how to dispose of his brothers and sisters, using trickery to bring about their deaths in a merciless pursuit of power. A younger brother, Ayca, becomes the god of farming and is content with dominion over plants rather than people. Manco builds his palace and marries his eldest sister Mama Ocllo, and from this union he founds the Inca nation.

Cuzco – the historic capital of the Inca empire from the 13th to 16th centuries.

Ceremony in the Inca capital of Cuzco: Manco Cápac (Ayar Manco) confers distinction on the Princes of the Blood by piercing their ears, shown in a 19th-century engraving from Usi e costumi di tutti i popoli dell'Universo.

BLURRING HISTORY, LEGEND AND MYTHOLOGY

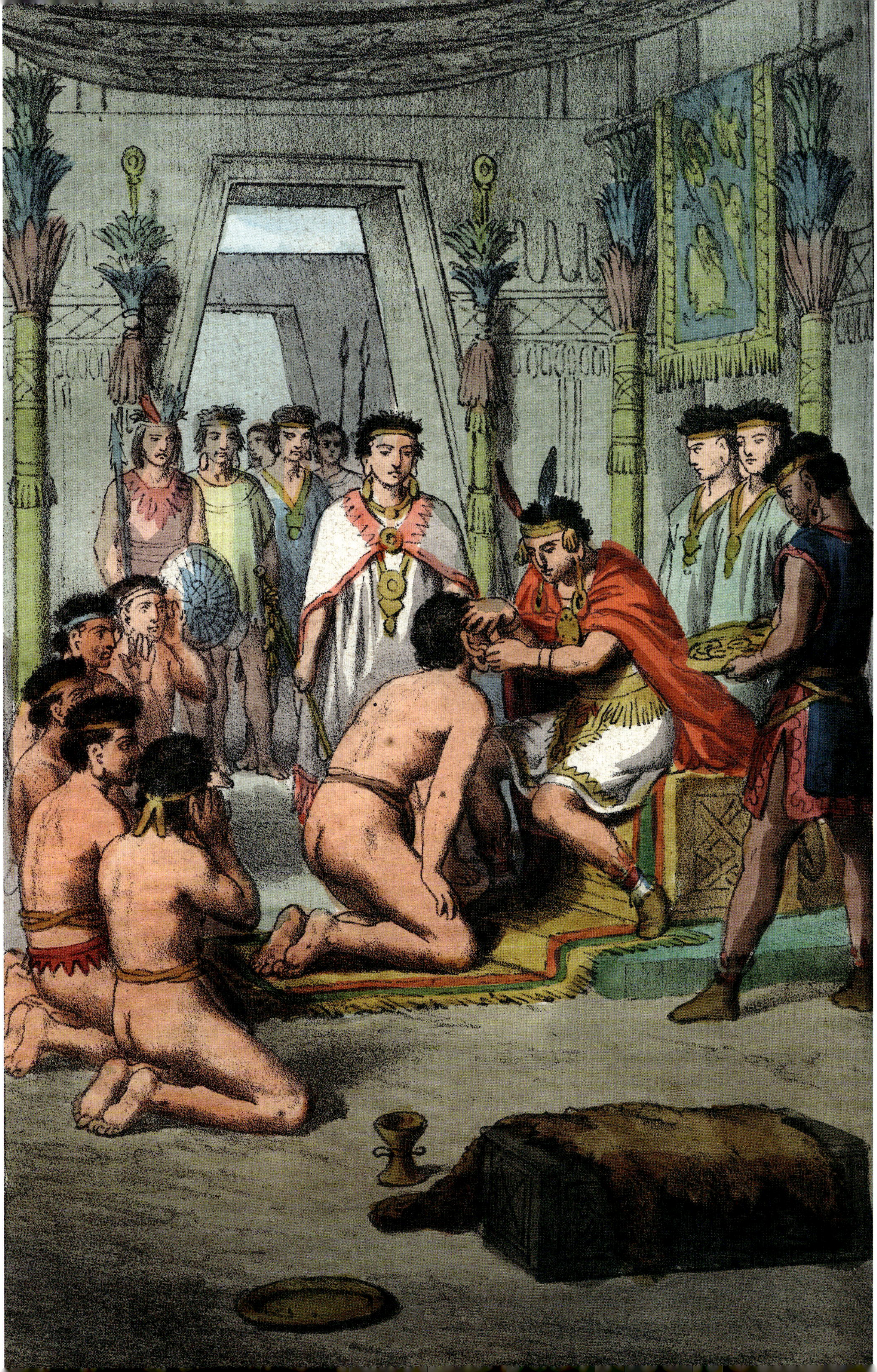

KING ARTHUR
BRITAIN

King Arthur is a semi-legendary British leader who is said to have led Britons against Saxon invaders in the 5th and 6th centuries. The existence of King Arthur is much debated. Some historians believe that he was a real Romano-British warrior leader or king. Others say there is not enough evidence to prove he actually existed, but admit that Britons of the past revered him as a legendary figurehead.

King Arthur and his knights at the Round Table, shown here in a wood engraving after a 14th-century medieval miniature. The Norman chronicler Wace was the first to mentions the Round Table, in his Roman de Brut of 1155. There, he simply says that Arthur devised the idea to prevent quarrels between his barons over the question of precedence.

BLURRING HISTORY, LEGEND AND MYTHOLOGY

Le Mont-Saint-Michel, Normandy, France, where Arthur is supposed to have slain a dragon.

The most famous stories in Arthurian mythology, including those of Camelot, Merlin, the Lady in the Lake and the Holy Grail, were not recorded until the 12th century. It is possible that they existed in oral tradition before then.

In the classic version, King Uther Pendragon seduces his enemy's wife, resulting in the birth of the illegitimate Arthur. Uther dies without legitimate heir, and there is much disagreement over who should be the next king. To decide the issue the wizard Merlin embeds a sword in a large stone; it is agreed that whoever can pull the sword from the stone will be the next king. Many try, but none succeed until a young Arthur pulls the sword from the stone by mistake, without realizing its significance. As a consequence, he becomes king.

King Arthur's sword is called Excalibur and has magical powers. In some stories, Excalibur is the weapon he pulls from the stone, but in most legends the sword Excalibur is forged on the island of Avalon. It is the Lady of the Lake, the ruler of Avalon, who gives the sword to King Arthur. When Arthur dies it is returned to her.

Merlin and Arthur are inextricably linked in Arthurian legend. The magician and wise man from Welsh mythology acts as Arthur's mentor throughout his reign. Merlin is also credited with the idea of a Round Table, around which all King Arthur's knights gather, so that all have equal status.

According to legend, it is after the Romans leave ancient Britain and Saxon invaders flood into the island that Arthur comes to prominence. The Britons are facing defeat at the Battle of Mount Badon when Arthur rallies his troops and leads the Britons to victory. It is in this period of peace that the mythology develops, portraying Arthur as a victor and the creator of the stronghold of Camelot.

Camelot is both a castle and a court that is associated with King Arthur, portrayed as his realm and a symbol of the Arthurian world. His knights, including Lancelot and Gawain, meet around the Round Table. Many places have been suggested as the location of the original Camelot, including South Cadbury, near Glastonbury, in the Somerset marshes, and St Michael's Mount in Cornwall. King Arthur is said to have killed a dragon on France's Mont-Saint-Michel.

King Arthur's final battle is against Mordred, sometimes said to be his illegitimate son, at a place called Camlann. Arthur dies in the battle and his body is taken to its final resting place on the island of Avalon.

THE ULSTER CYCLE AND FENIAN CYCLE
IRELAND

The history of Ireland is based around four cycles of Celtic mythology and mixes legendary and historical events, even attaching specific dates to stories that must surely be mythological. The first one, the Mythological Cycle, and the final one, the Historical Cycle, are self-explanatory, so we know what degree of authenticity to expect. However, the accuracy of the middle two cycles, the Ulster and the Fenian, are decidedly more blurred.

The Ulster Cycle (also the Ulaid Cycle) tells of the heroic age of the Ulaids, people from the northeast of Ireland from whom the modern name for the province, 'Ulster', is derived. The stories, set in the 1st century AD, are based on oral tradition and recorded between the 8th and 11th centuries. They were preserved in manuscript form in the 12th century.

These manuscripts include *The Book of the Dun Cow* (c.1100), *The Book of Leinster* (c.1160) and, later, *The Yellow Book of Lecan* (14th century). In these tales mythological elements intermingle with more clearly historical details.

The tales and legends are set in a pre-Christian time, and tell of druids and of battling aristocrats fighting on chariots. The stories also feature conflict between the men of Ulster and Connaught, a father-son duel, beheadings, and romance. Most of the stories are short prose narratives.

The Fenian Cycle (also the Fionn or the Ossianic Cycle) centres on the legendary hero Finn mac Cumhaill (MacCool) and his band of warriors (the Fianna Eireann) in the 3rd century. Again, the tales and legends were passed down orally before being recorded in the 12th century.

The outstanding manuscript of this cycle is *The Interrogation of the Old Men* (1200) and stories were also

Finn mac Cumhaill Comes to Aid the Fianna, *an illustration by Stephen Reid, 1932.*

BLURRING HISTORY, LEGEND AND MYTHOLOGY

The Giant's Causeway on the coast of Northern Ireland is a unique landmark of hexagonal basalt rock coloums. According to legend, Finn mac Cumhaill built these rocks as stepping stones to Scotland. Finn is often portrayed as a benevolent giant responsible for creating various geographical features in Ireland.

included in *The Book of Dun Cow* and *The Book of Leinster*.

The Fenian Cycle is less violent and turbulent than the Ulster Cycle that precedes it, but still contains tales of battles and adventures. The Fenian Cycle's themes include hunting, romance and wisdom, and draw comparisons with the Arthurian legends.

Finn ('The Fair') is a descendant of the druids who is raised in the forest after his father, chief of the Fianna, is killed. Finn grows up to be a great warrior who avenges his father's killing and becomes head of the Fianna. The tales also deal with Finn's son Oisín and grandson Oscar, as well as other members of the Fianna. One such is the handsome Diarmaid (Dermot) who eventually brings about the group's downfall. Diarmaid elopes with Princess Grainne who Finn, by then an old man, wants to marry. When Diarmaid is later injured, Finn denies him water and he dies. This action prompts the king of Ireland to take up arms against the Fianna, who are defeated at the battle of Gabhra.

The Ulster Cycle and Fenian Cycle

Bran the Blessed
Britain

Bran the Blessed is a semi-human giant in Welsh mythology. He is the son of the sea god, Llyr, and the maternal grandson of the sun god, Belenos. 'Bran' means 'Raven' in ancient Welsh and this bird is his symbol.

Bran is of enormous size and strength and is in possession of magical powers. He has a cauldron that can restore the dead to life.

The first known reference to Bran the Blessed appears in the story of 'Branwen Daughter of Llyr' in the *Mabinogion*. Branwen is Bran's sister.

Branwen marries Matholwch, the King of Ireland, and bears him a son, Gwern. For a time, unity and peace between the two nations seem possible. However, after Bran and Branwen's jealous half-brother, Efnysien, insults Matholwch by mutilating his horses, the fragile peace is in jeopardy. Bran gives Matholwch the magic cauldron of rebirth as recompense, however Matholwch begins to mistreat Branwen, beating her daily. She sends a starling with a message asking her brother for help and Bran responds by gathering his army and setting off across the Irish Sea to save her.

Due to his giant size, Bran can easily wade across the sea, but his army isn't as fortunate. So, Bran lies down and forms a bridge across the sea, which his army uses to get across. The Irish eventually agree to make peace, until Efnysien unexpectedly murders Gwern by throwing him into a fire. Conflict erupts again and Branwen dies of grief. Knowing that the Irish are using the cauldron of rebirth to regenerate his warriors, Bran destroys the cauldron from within and, in the process, fatally wounds himself. As he lies dying, Bran asks for his head to be buried at 'White Hill' in London, facing the continent, to guard against invaders. However, at a later date, King Arthur declares he does not need Bran's head to look out for him and orders it to be dug up and removed.

The 'White Hill', where Bran's head was buried, is thought to be the site of the Tower of London.

BLURRING HISTORY, LEGEND AND MYTHOLOGY

Branwen tames a starling to send a message to her brother so that she might be rescued from her husband Matholwch, the cruel King of Ireland.

The bridge Bran formed is said to symbolize his link between this world and the otherworld. He has been given the epithet 'The Blessed' as he is credited with bringing Christianity to Britain. The symbol of the raven is still prominent today in British mythology, with ravens being kept in the Tower of London. It is said that if the ravens were ever to fly away, Britain would fall to invaders.

ROMULUS AND REMUS
ITALY

In Roman legend, Romulus and Remus are twins: sons of Rhea and either Hercules or Mars. They are descendants of Aeneas on their mother's side and famed as the founders of Rome.

A 16th-century etching depicting Romulus and Remus building the walls of Rome.

Rhea is a Vestal Virgin who has taken a vow of chastity, so when she gives birth to twins, she is punished for breaking her vow. The usual sentence for this crime is the killing of the woman and her child. However, King Amulius, fearing the wrath of the paternal god (Hercules or Mars), decides to imprison Rhea instead. Her twins are given to a servant to drown in the river, but the servant spares their lives and sets them afloat in a basket on the Tiber River.

The river god Tibernus calms the river and so ensures the boys' safety. Their basket gets caught up in the roots of a fig tree, and they are discovered by a she-wolf who suckles them through infancy. The twins are then adopted by a shepherd and his wife, and become shepherds themselves.

One day, while herding their sheep, the twins encounter some of King Amulius' shepherds, who start a fight in which Remus is captured. Romulus gathers a band of local shepherds and sets off to save his brother. King Amulius does not recognize Rhea's sons, as he believes her twins to be dead. Romulus kills King Amulius and frees his brother.

Romulus and Remus leave their homeland and set off in search of a place to build their own city. However, they quarrel over where to build it. Romulus wants to build the city on the Palatine Hill, while Remus prefers the Aventine Hill. They settle the argument through augury, a type of prophecy involving the sighting of birds. Remus sees six auspicious birds and Romulus sees twelve, so Romulus thinks he has won. However Remus says he saw the birds first, which is more auspicious, so they still can't agree.

Romulus goes ahead and begins digging trenches and building walls on the Palatine Hill. Remus mocks the walls his brother has made. Angered by this, Romulus kills Remus.

After burying his brother, Romulus continues to build his city, which he names Roma, after himself. Initially, the city is mainly populated by fugitives, criminals and runaway slaves and there is a shortage of females. To solve this problem, Romulus invites the neighbouring Sabine men to a festival and, while they are preoccupied, his men abduct their women. Romulus forces the women to marry Romans, compensating them with 'lawful wedlock' and full rights to all civil priviledges, for both them and their children.

Titus Tatius, the Sabine king, launches a full-scale attack on Rome that the Romans almost lose. After much bloodshed, the Sabine women eventually intervene, demanding peace for the sake of their children. A truce is declared and the two kings, Tatius and Romulus, rule Rome jointly for five years until the two fall out and Tatius is banished. Romulus now becomes sole king of Rome, an ever-expanding empire that soon includes his original homeland. Romulus reigns for twenty years until his death.

There is much debate over whether Romulus and Remus existed or were purely mythological. While some of the stories told about them are clearly fanciful, many scholars believe they could be based on historical figures.

One of the mosaics on the floor of Galleria Vittorio Emanuele II, Milan, representing Rome (the she-wolf and Romulus and Remus).

The Founding of Athens
Greece

Athens is the capital city of Greece and has been inhabited for more than 7000 years, with over 3400 years of recorded history. It has long been renowned for its literature, buildings, arts and education. For thousands of years, people have visited Athens from all over the world to live or to trade. The city continues to be referred to as the cradle of Western civilization and the birthplace of democracy.

In Greek mythology, the first settlement was built on the rock of Acropolis in 3000BC. The naming of Athens is settled after a competition between the goddess of wisdom, Athena, and the god of the sea, Poseidon, over who is to be protector of the city. To decide the issue, Zeus says that the two gods must each make an offering to the city. Athena offers the people an olive tree. Poseidon offers them a spring of sea water, by striking a rock with his trident. The people prefer Athena's gift and so choose her as their protector, and so the city is named after her. To this day, many of Athena's olive trees can be found in the suburbs of Athens. The Athenians have also dedicated many temples to her, and still organize festivals to honour her. When official currency was introduced, the coins featured Athena and her sacred bird, the owl, symbol of wisdom.

According to legend, the first king of Athens is Cecrops, a man with a human upper body and a serpent or fish-tail lower body. It is Cecrops who judges Athena to be the winner of the competition with Poseidon. He is the first of a line of kings who ruled Athens until around the 12th century BC. During the time of these kings, the city grows in power and influence, incorporating the surrounding settlements of Attica, the historical region surrounding Athens.

Statue of Athena, goddess of philosophy and wisdom.

BLURRING HISTORY, LEGEND AND MYTHOLOGY

Cecrops, the mythical founding king of Athens, depicted on a ceramic plate from Attica, c.440BC. His upper half is human and his bottom half is shown as a serpent or fish-tail.

This is the same dynasty that also presides over the famous years of conflict with Troy (see pages 174-5), but is eventually replaced by Dorian culture and language when Melanthus takes the kingship of Athens, an event known as the 'Return of the Heracleidae' - the decendents of Heracles.

Athens is also an important setting for many Greek myths and legends. The Aegean Sea is named after King Aegeus who leaps to his death after he mistakenly believes his son Theseus has been killed by the Minotaur in Crete (see also page 128).

King Menestheus, another king of Athens, plays an integral part in the legends of the Trojan War. He is one of the suitors of Helen of Troy and is also one of the warriors who hides in the Trojan Horse and participates in the sacking of Troy (see also pages 174-5).

The founding of Athens

WOLF, MOTHER OF THE TURKS
TURKEY

Turkic mythology has developed from numerous cultural influences and is rich with a multiplicity of approaches and stories. The mythology embraces elements of shamanism, and has been influenced by Buddhism and Zoroastrianism. With the arrival of Islam, threads from that faith and history have also been incorporated. There are similarities with the Greek and Finno-Ugric myth systems, too.

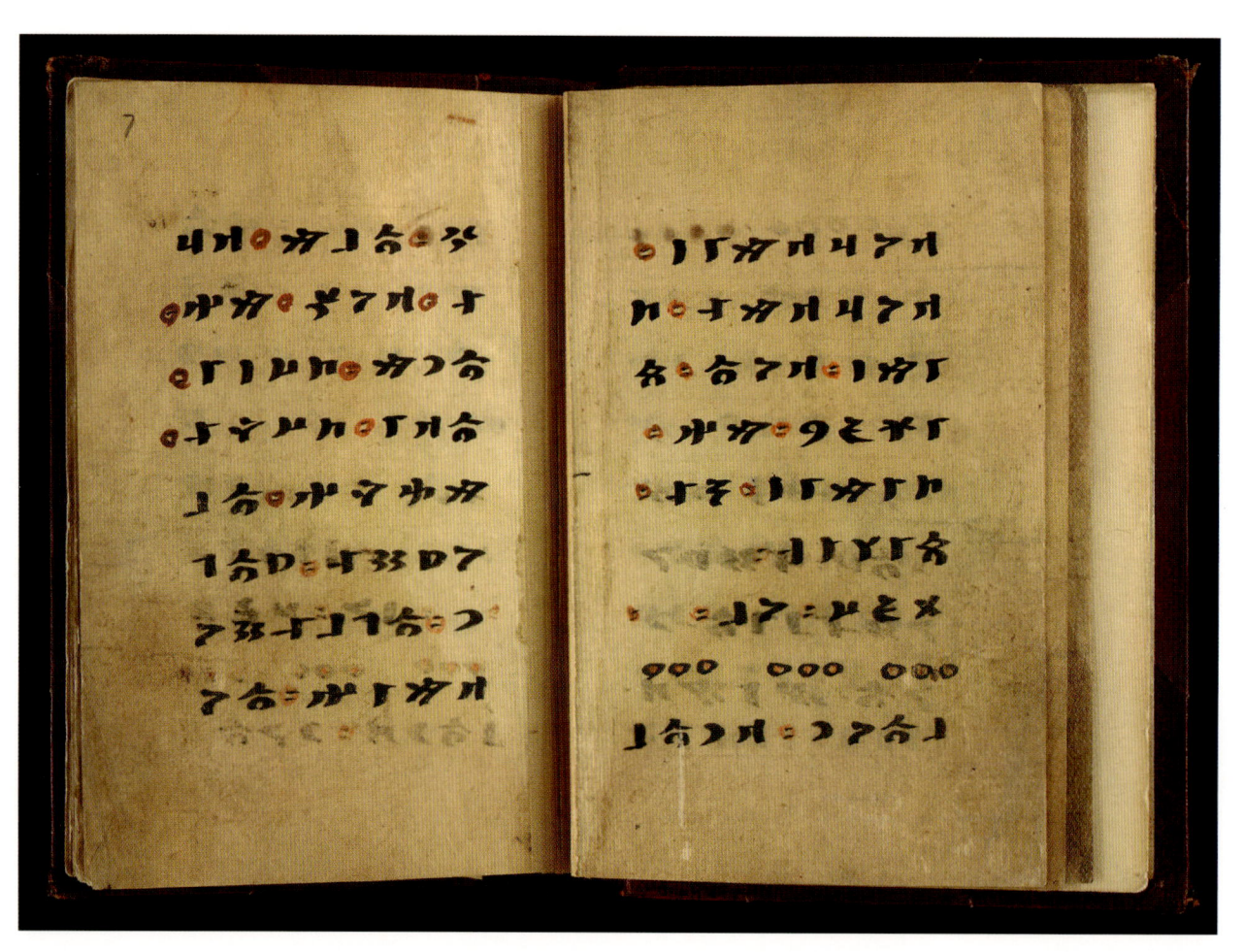

Pages from The Book of Omens (Irk Bitig)*, written in the 10th century.*

In the Turkic mythological world, the wolf, symbolizing honour, is considered the mother of the Turkish people. *The Book of Omens (Irk Bitig)*, written in the 10th century, is the most important manuscript yet discovered concerning Turkish mythology.

The legend of the blue wolf involves a young boy who is the sole survivor following a series of battles and raids on Turkey. A blue she-wolf named Asena finds the child and nurses him back to health. When he is older, he impregnates the wolf and she gives birth to ten half-wolf, half-human sons.

One of the sons, sometimes also called Asena, establishes the Ashina clan of Göktürks, with a wolf's head as its emblem. It is the ruling dynasty of a coalition of Turkish nomadic empires in medieval inner Asia. These people ultimately migrate to the Altai region in today's Siberia.

BLURRING HISTORY, LEGEND AND MYTHOLOGY

A stamp printed in Turkey shows a blacksmith and grey wolf. According to the myth, the first Turks who migrated to the Altai region were known for their skill as blacksmiths.

Asena the wolf is a symbol of Turkey's cultural identity and was considered to be featured on the nation's coat of arms in 1925. Asena's image is embossed on the stage of the personal theatre of the first President of Turkey, Mustafa Kemal Atatürk, at his residence in Ankara.

Viracocha and the founding of Cuzco — Peru

Viracocha is the supreme god of the Incas who formed the heavens, earth, sun, moon, and all living beings. He is the father of all the other Inca gods. His alternative spellings of his name include Huiracocha and Wiraqoca/ Wiracocha.

Viracocha Gate of the Sun, Kalasasaya Temple in Tiahuanaco, Bolivia.

Viracocha was first worshipped by the pre-Inca people of Peru, and then incorporated into the Inca pantheon. In Inca mythology, Viracocha gave weapons and a headdress to Manco Capac, the legendary warrior and founder of the Inca Dynasty.

Viracocha succeeds in creating humans only on the second attempt. In his first attempt, he creates a race of giants from stone. They are so unruly that he has to send a great flood to wipe them out. His second, successful, attempt involves the use of clay to create man and woman. He then creates the sun to give them light, and teaches them agriculture, language and the arts. This creation starts on the islands around Lake Titicaca.

Manco Capac is one of the first Incas to be created. He emerges from the underworld (or Lake Titicaca) and sets about finding a place to build a city and start a civilization. He has a golden staff and Viracocha tells him that wherever he can sink his staff into the ground without resistance is the place he should start building.

He chooses a site in a basin surrounded by mountain peaks, where three rivers meet. In Inca style, nature is not destroyed but incorporated into the layout of

The ruins of Raqch'i, or Temple of Wiracocha, in the Cusco region of Peru.

the city. After Viracocha has finished his creation, he travels the world teaching humanity and art. He is disguised as a beggar called Kon-Tiki and is not always well received. In his absence, lesser deities are given the duty of looking after mankind's interests, although Viracocha is always watching from afar.

The god's name was assumed by the king known as Viracocha Inca, who died in 1438. This may be the time that Viracocha was formally added to the pantheon of Inca gods.

There were temples dedicated to Viracocha at the Inca capital of Peru, Cuzco, as well as at Caha and Urcos. Human and animal sacrifices were made to the god at important Inca ceremonies.

THE JADE EMPEROR
CHINA

The Jade Emperor is also known as the August Personage of Jade, Father-Heaven, or Yudi.

In Chinese mythology, he is the supreme deity and ruler of the heavens. He rules his heaven as the earthly emperor rules China; the Chinese conception of gods is based on Chinese bureaucracy. Human beings who lead exemplary lives enter the Jade Emperor's heaven after death.

The Jade Emperor is one of the first gods, credited with crafting the first humans from clay. Some claim there is no god involved in creation, and give credit to the union of matter and movement (*yin* and *yang*).

The gods of the Court of the Jade Emperor are important deities who were worshipped throughout China. Other important gods included Mazu ('Empress of Heaven') and Guan Yu (linked to warfare and military valour).

The Jade Emperor originates in ancient Chinese oral mythology, but was officially incorporated into Chinese religion in 1007 by Emperor Shenzong in the Song Dynasty after he claimed to have seen the Jade Emperor in a dream.

The Jade Emperor lives in a palace just like the earthly Emperor's, and his court, officers and soldiers are organized exactly as they are on earth.

The Queen Mother Wang is the Jade Emperor's wife. Her name is thought to be a corruption of the Lady-Queen of the West, found in the 4th-century narrative *The Romance of the Emperor Mu*. Ancient legends tell of her living in the K'un-lum mountains, the abode of the immortals. Popular legend suggests she lives in the palace of the Jade Emperor with her attendants, in the highest level of heaven.

In Beijing, at the Temple of Heaven, two sacrifices were made to the Jade Emperor each year, one in the winter solstice and one in spring.

Yuhuang Dadi, the Jade Emperor, supreme deity of Daoism.

BLURRING HISTORY, LEGEND AND MYTHOLOGY

Nansha Tianhou Temple, with a statue of Boddhisatva Mazu, Empress of Heaven.

The Temple of Heaven in Beijing. Traditionally, two annual sacrifices were made to the Jade Emperor each year, one in the winter solstice and one in spring.

The Jade Emperor

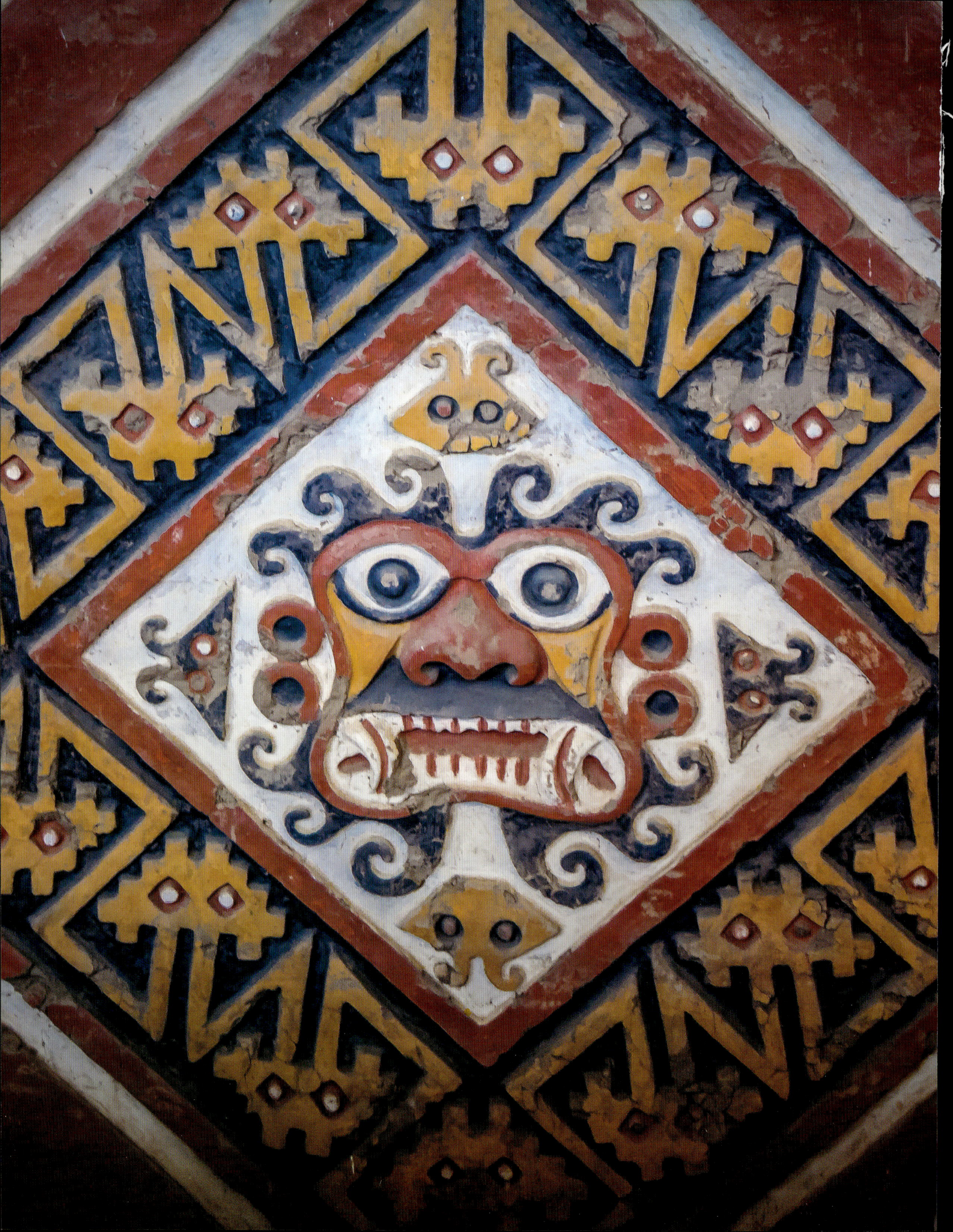

Customs and popular religion

There have been many unusual alliances and twists and turns when the belief systems of different cultures came together. Often colonialism forced indigenous religions to be absorbed or to coincide with the dominant belief systems of the oppressors. In some cases, appealing aspects of other cultures and customs have been appropriated or fetishized by more modern practitioners from other societies. These clashes of beliefs have resulted in versions of ancient customs that persist to this day.

Vision quests
North America

A vision quest is a rite of passage traditionally undertaken by young boys at the time of puberty. These quests are best known among the Great Plains Indian tribes of North America. Preparation for a vision quest involves fasting, isolation, prayer and meditation. It leaves the quester feeling physically tired but mentally refreshed. It is conducted in a place of natural beauty with minimal distractions so that the individual can appreciate the wildlife and attempt to free the mind of trivial thoughts.

Scars of the Sun Dance

In certain tribes, such as the Pawnee, Mandan and Sioux, the vision quest is called 'crying for a vision'. The rigorous physical challenges include exposing yourself to the elements and slashing your body.

In addition to self-harm, some tribes include torture and hallucinogens in their vision quests. The Sun Dance of the Plains Indians involves four days of solitary experience, exposed to the sun during the day and the cold at night, followed by being hung up by ropes and animal claws. Their vision quest scars are a sign that they have undertaken the difficult Sun Dance ritual.

A Thirst or Sun Dance by Cree Indians in northwest Canada.

A vision quest is an attempt to see a vision of a future guardian spirit. A quest can also be performed by someone wishing to seek a power animal to guide and protect them through different stages of their life. The quests are based on the idea of animism (see page 230-1): that all natural objects in the universe have souls or spirits. A vision quest is also called a 'spiritual journey' and sometimes associated with a trance-like state or an out-of-body experience. During the quest of up to three days of solitude, a power song is prepared to be sung or chanted by each person. The quest is followed by feasting and celebrations.

A man hangs during a suspension show at Cool Inc. Tattoo Convention in Johannesburg, South Africa. Previously a practice used by Native Americans to achieve visions and out-of-body experiences through creating an altered physical state, body suspension and other forms of body modifications have been adopted into modern subcultures.

Vision quests

Feng Shui

China

Feng Shui is an ancient art and science, developed in China over 3,000 years ago and still practised today. It concerns awareness of how to position furniture in a home, office or garden to balance energies and bring good fortune.

It is believed that Feng Shui can assist in many aspects of an individual's life, such as money, health, career and romance. Feng Shui can be described simply as the interaction between humans and their environment.

The word 'feng' means 'wind' and 'shui' means 'water'. In classical Chinese culture, these elements are associated with good health. Wind and water are the basic requirements for human survival and the two fundamental and flowing elements in the universe. Wind and water are direct carriers of *chi*: the life force or energy.

Feng Shui practitioners believe that the placement of things and objects in your physical space influences the energy flow of the space, which in turn affects your own personal energy flow and so determines how you will perform.

There are five elements of Feng Shui: wood, fire, earth, water and metal. Those elements interact in different ways, and are called the Productive and Destructive cycles.

A 17th-century Chinese dish showing sages with the yin-yang symbol, used for divination.

CUSTOMS AND POPULAR RELIGION

An ancient Chinese Feng Shui compass.

The *yin-yang* theory is key in Taoist cosmology, including Feng Shui. The principle behind *yin* and *yang* is that everything in the universe is composed of two opposing, but deeply connected, forces – feminine energy (*yin*) and masculine energy (*yang*). In Feng Shui, feminine energy is black and masculine energy is white.

Some historians have claimed that Neanderthal cavemen nearly 30,000 years ago practised Feng Shui as they chose their caves based on three principles: they were on high ground, easily seen and close to water. Those three principles continue to underlie the basic principles of 'modern' Feng Shui. The energy or *chi* that flows through the universe flows through the individual and the local environment.

Feng Shui

Animism
World mythologies

Animism is the oldest known belief system in the world. The name comes from the Latin *anima*, meaning 'breath, spirit, life'. Animism is the belief that all natural objects have souls that can exist separately from their physical bodies. Thus, everything in nature, such as animals, plants, rivers and mountains, contains an inner spiritual essence.

These spirits can either help or harm humans, so they must be worshipped. Animists offer sacrifices, prayers and dances to the spirits. Because of a belief that all living things are equal, animists believe that plants and animals must be treated respectfully; a central concern is the correct way to eat animals and plants or to use them in other ways to satisfy human needs. As an example, Maori communities in New Zealand offer incantations or prayers (*karakias*) to their sweet potatoes as they pull them from the earth, to acknowledge that they have equal rights to the land and arrived at the same time as the people.

The Karen people of northern Thailand believe there are spirits in the houses, fields, water, rice, buffalo and trees and much else. They must all be given sacrifices of food to keep them happy and minimize the risk that they will cause trouble to humans.

Although animism comes in many forms, the concept runs like a thread through the spiritual belief systems of many different indigenous peoples. The concept is so deeply ingrained that most indigenous languages do not even have a word for animism.

A patung, or statue, in Kalimantan, Indonesian Borneo. Such statues are used by the Dayak peoples for remembrance of ancestors, keeping evil spirits at bay and for tethering buffalo to during sacrificial ceremonies. This patung has a spirit animal on its head.

People in costumes and decorated ghost masks at the annual Phi Ta Khon (Ghosts in Masks) festival in Dansai, Loei Province, Thailand.

Divination and fortune-telling
World mythologies

Divination is the practice of seeking knowledge of the future or the unknown by supernatural means. It describes any action that gathers information directly from the divine, often through the use of interpretive tools. Fortune tellers, however, believe their ability to predict a person's future is innate and, unlike divination, they do not require divine guidance. People who have the ability to see into the future by whatever means go by different names, including seer, soothsayer, clairvoyant, oracle and augur. For example, in Roman mythology, twin brothers Romulus and Remus consulted augurs when trying to decide where to build the city of Rome.

Fortune-telling scene and signs of the Chinese zodiac, reproduced in Recherche sur les superstitions en Chine *by Father Henri Doré, 1911.*

Predicting the future from reading coffee grounds, engraved by Charles William Sharpe (1818–99).

In the West, fortune-telling is most closely associated with the Romany people, first appearing in the 15th and 16th centuries. Divination arose from non-Western cultures such as China, especially with the *I Ching*, an ancient divination text. This became popular in the West in the 19th and 20th centuries. Divination and fortune-telling are areas ripe for fraud, often involving tenuous links and generalized predictions. Many organized religions oppose fortune-telling and divination based on various scriptural prohibitions.

Huacas: monuments of holiness
South America

In the ancient Inca and modern Quechuan languages of South America, a *huaca* (also *wak'a*) is a monument of some kind that represents a revered object or set of objects. The word huaca means 'sacredness' or 'holiness'.

A huaca can be a natural object, such as a huge rock, or a man-made shrine. A traditional belief among the Quechua people is that every object has a physical presence and two spirits (*camaquen*). One of these spirits created the object and the other animated it.

Huacas are found throughout the original Inca territory from Ecuador to Chile and can be as simple as a pile of stones or as complex as carved, stepped pyramids. There are more pyramid structures in the Americas than in the rest of the world combined. Some huacas are built along a processional ceremonial line. These

Huaca de la Luna archaeological complex, near Trujillo, La Libertad Province, Peru.

Detail of the ancient wall at Huaca de la Luna in Trujillo, Peru.

lines are called *ceques*. They are laid out to express the cosmology of the culture, and often aligned to astronomical or seasonal ceremonies.

In the Trujillo area of Peru, there are two temples standing adjacent to each other: Huaca del Sol (Temple of the Sun) and Huaca del Luna (Temple of the Moon). Collectively they are known as Huacas del Moche. Of the two pyramids, Huaca del Sol is the larger; indeed it is the largest adobe structure in the Americas. The twin temples are located on what is thought to be the most important ceremonial centre for the Moche culture at its peak, AD400–600. Although Huaca del Sol appears as a huge structure to today's visitors, only around a third of it can actually be seen.

Earth mound

Approximately 500 kilometres (310 miles) northwest of Lima, on the northern Peruvian coast, you can find a large and complex stone and earth platform mound 32 metres (105 feet) high on the site of a prehistoric settlement called Huaca Prieta. The settlement is named after the organically rich dark earth that characterizes the site.

Huacas: monuments of holiness

Quetzalcoatl as an incarnation of Jesus

Mesoamerica

Quetzalcoatl is the god of wind and wisdom in Mesoamerican mythology. His name, which means 'feathered serpent', comes from the Aztec Nahuatl language.

This deity is most often depicted as a feathered serpent, but sometimes he is shown as a white man, looking nothing like the people who worship him. In this case, he is known as 'white bearded god'.

The Church of Jesus Christ of Latter-day Saints is considered by its Mormon followers to be the restoration of the original church founded by Jesus Christ. Some members of the Mormon faith believe that the depiction of Quetzalcoatl as a white-bearded god is actually an incarnation of Jesus Christ. In the Book of Mormon, Jesus is said to have visited Native American people after his resurrection.

Jesus appears to the Nephites. According to the Book of Mormon, the Nephites are one of four groups of people who migrated from Jerusalem to the ancient Americas in Biblical times. The Mormons believe that after his time in the Middle East, Jesus visited America to teach and heal the chosen people there.

CUSTOMS AND POPULAR RELIGION

Quetzalcoatl, the feathered serpent, is shown here with a bright background in the Aztec style.

This idea is much debated among Mormons. Some believe that revering a 'feathered serpent' constitutes snake worship, which would be inconsistent with Christian worship. But others believe snakes play an important role in the Bible, with the brass serpent placed on a pole and raised up by Moses given as an example.

Those who believe Quetzalcoatl is Jesus Christ give the following as evidence:
- Mesoamericans believed Quetzalcoatl is the creator of life
- Mesoamericans believed he is the greatest Lord of all
- Mesoamericans believed Quetzalcoatl will return
- Quetzalcoatl teaches virtue
- Quetzalcoatl has a long beard and the features of a white man

Those who do not believe this say the following about Quetzalcoatl:
- He is linked to snake worship
- Human sacrifice was made to him
- He had a twin brother (Xolotl)

A feathered serpent god is not unique to the Aztecs. In many ancient Mesoamerican cultures there is a feathered serpent god who, along with his men, is tall with a white skin and a beard. This god is called Viracocha by the Inca (see also pages 220–1) and Kukulkan by the Maya.

Quetzalcoatl as an incarnation of Jesus

Witchcraft and sorcery
World mythologies

Witchcraft and sorcery are widely considered to be similar practices as both use magic spells and mystical or paranormal means to harness occult forces in order to produce the desired results. However, they are both complex concepts with many varied definitions.

Salem witch trials: a woman protests as one of her accusers, a young girl, appears to have convulsions. A small group of women were the source of accusations, testimony and dramatic demonstrations.

Witchcraft is defined as the practice of magic, especially 'black magic', including the use of spells for good and ill. It is generally considered to result from inherent mystical powers that cannot be learned. Sorcery, on the other hand, is seen as a form of magic that can be learned and practised by anyone.

Witchcraft as a concept varies widely between different cultures. In some societies it is considered to be an ancient religion, quite separate from other practices such as shamanism, nature worship, superstition and sorcery.

Traditionally, a female practitioner of witchcraft is known as a witch and a male practitioner as a wizard, although today 'witch' can be used for both genders. In sorcery, the female is known as a sorceress and the male as a sorcerer.

Both witchcraft and sorcery have existed for millennia in societies and cultures around the world. There are several references to witches in ancient Roman and Greek mythology, and in the Bible.

Although witches have often been persecuted, the tradition known as Wiccan has been practised around the world as a religion that involves no harm to others, with a belief in karma and a connection with Mother Nature.

The witch Baba Yaga, illustration by Ivan Bilibin, 1900.

Vodou
West Africa

Vodou (sometimes spelt Voodoo, Vodoun, Vodun or Vodu) is still practised around the world. The basic features of Vodou were transported from West Africa, particularly Benin, with the slave trade. In Vodou belief, nature is controlled entirely by spiritual forces, which must be acknowledged and honoured through sacred offerings and animal sacrifice. Practitioners enter a state of ecstatic trance as a means of communication with the gods and spirits. Magical practices play an important role in the ritual. When slaves settled in the New World, some Christian elements began to be introduced into Vodou practices. Sometimes African deities take on aspects of some of the saints. At various times attempts have been made to suppress Vodou, but it has survived and continues to flourish in many parts of the world.

Statues covered with oil and blood inside a Vodou temple for a ceremony, in Bohicon, Benin, West Africa.

Le Baron Samedi, Vodou pearl flag, Port-au-Prince, Haiti.

There are two main branches of Vodou outside of West Africa: Haitian Vodou and New Orleans Vodou. In Haiti, Vodou has been the official national religion since 1993. Haitian Vodou is an African diasporic religion: an amalgamation of several tribes (including Yoruba and Fon) who were forced together in slavery. There are also aspects of French Catholicism in Haitian Vodou. For example, the images of Catholic saints are used to honour the *lwa* (spirits). The lwa were Rada Lwa (from the Fon and Yoruba), the Petwo Lwa (spirits of the Congo, the Taino and modern Haitians) and the Gede Lwa (spirits of the dead). The language of Haitian Vodou is Kreyol (the local dialect of French).

The lwa each serve different purposes and are prayed to when people are in need of a specific type of help. There are male and female lwa, and the females are as important as the males. Many Vodou communities are led by female priestesses.

In West African Vodou, there are three ranks of ancestral spirits: the founders of the clans, those who died before genealogical records were kept, and the known, or recent, dead.

New Orleans Vodou includes some of the lwa found in Haitian Vodou, but Catholic saints also have a strong presence. The primary liturgical language used is English.

Haiti's national religion, as with so many world religions, is a rich cultural expression of a people with a strong and tragic history, one including successful resistance to oppression. The ancestral traditions prevail and continue to sustain the people in the face of adversity. The religion remains something of an enigma, with a perverse and misconstrued history.

Ancestor worship
World mythologies

Ancestor worship is not a religion in itself, but rather a religious practice still carried out by people across different cultures and religions. It is based on the belief that the spirits of deceased family members continue to care for their family and influence the fortunes of the living. The spirits of ancestors are also thought to act as mediators between the living and the creator.

Ancestor worship remains at the core of religious practices in China, Africa, Malaysia and Polynesia. It is a type of worship that is traced back to ancient Romans and Egyptians. Its two main principles are the belief that those who have gone before have a continuing interest in the living. There is the fear that the dead can still harm the living, so there is a need to placate them. The person to be venerated must have led a moral life with great social distinction, so there are controls applied to ancestor worship.

Among the American Pueblo Indians, the dead are believed to become one with their mythical forefathers, the *kachmas*. There are masked ceremonies and prayers to the departed asking them to bless the living with rain, happiness and fertility.

In China and Japan, the central tenet of ancestral worship is the belief in the wisdom of the elders and the importance of the continuity of the family. Religious practices are usually family affairs involving prayers and offerings in the home or temple.

A vintage engraving by Charles Fletcher Lummis from Pueblo Indian Folk-stories, 1910. *The image depicts Nah-chu-rú-chu, the Pueblo man who married the moon. Here he is grieving the death of his wife – who is later brough back to life.*

An unknown woman at the 15th annual Día de los Muertos *Festival (Day of the Dead) at the Hollywood Forever Cemetery in Los Angeles, California.*

Feng Shui (see pages 228-9) is taken into account when considering the placement of tombs and graves. Physical remains are laid to rest in this tomb, the site of public rituals, and an ancestral tablet representing the dead is place in the temple or on a shrine in the house.

Día de los Muertos (Day of the Dead) is an annual Mexican celebration with Mesoamerican roots. It celebrates the ancestors with honour and reverence. The ceremony is a bright and joyous affair, traditionally celebrated on the 1st or 2nd of November each year. Sugar and chocolate confectionery is made in the shape of skulls, people dress up in traditional costumes and there are parades on the street. The equivalent in countries with a Roman Catholic heritage, including France, Spain and Portugal, is All Saints Day. On that day people are given a day off work to visit cemeteries carrying candles and flowers as offerings for dead relatives.

The Day of the Dead parade in Paseo de la Reforma, Mexico City.

Ancestor worship   243

Conclusion

Whether you have read this book from beginning to end or simply leafed through its pages at random seeing what piques your interest, you will surely have marvelled at the creative enterprise that our forebears employed to make sense of their world. Today, we can relish how our cousins, across every strip of land on this planet, divined these intricate stories that have persisted for millennia and that originated in distant ages beyond our knowledge of recorded history.

It is a dizzying heritage we have, and it is surely no wonder that mythology still influences our modern imaginations, inspiring countless writers to revisit and bring back to life these historical treasures. To me, it is the commonality I discussed at the start of the book that is so puzzling. The parallels across these world mythologies reveal that every culture of peoples carried recognizable aspects of the story of humankind.

Throughout this book we have followed gods: gods of weather, agricultural gods; war gods and gods of death. Gods of love, too. These categories are strikingly similar across the span of the world and its centuries of occupation by humans. Sometimes, those gods take on more than one job, which can often seem at odds with their role. The productive work of a god who sets up an agricultural system and then does a little 'war god' work on the side sounds simply inexplicable. Where is the pride in that? But perhaps this dichotomy is quite a telling feature of our human psyche. One could argue that these binaries of production and growth, and destruction and senseless carnage, are part of the way we still experience the world today. Perhaps humans are hardwired to seek a justification for this kind of paradoxical behaviour?

We must remember that much of the mythological material we have inherited, shared, compared with other cultures and altered, was written by poets and carries large doses of knowledge spun out from human intuition rather than simply from observation and experience. Many symbols are contained in these narratives, so not everything can be understood literally. We can, however, admire the explanations these myths provide and the poetic turns of phrase that establish for us an ordered version of existence – helpfully resolving how we have made the transition from primordial chaos to a world we recognize as home and that offers some sense of structure.

Being firmly rooted in an age of science and technology, it is easy for us to be critical of, and even to deride, the fantastical aspects of the belief systems of our progenitors. We can forget just how powerful a profoundly inspiring story was to earlier cultures where storytellers were revered and narrative was the epitome of invention. But while we may be more sceptical of this sort of invention today, our lives are still heavily governed by stories. Whether it be the news we receive from the media, the political ideologies we subscribe to or the theories we glean from science, our need for narrative is not so different from that of our ancestors.

BIBILIOGRAPHY

Brogan, T., & Preminger, A. (1993). *The New Princeton Encyclopedia of Poetry and Poetics.*
Princeton, N.J.: Princeton University Press.

Burn, L. (1990). *Greek Myths.* Hyderabad: Orient Blackswan.

Dell, C. (2012). *Mythology: An Illustrated Journey into our Imagined Worlds.*
London: Thames and Hudson.

Graves, R. et al (1959). *New Larousse Encyclopedia of Mythology.* London: Hamlyn.

Grimal, P. (1986). *A Concise Dictionary of Classical Mythology.*
Oxford, Basil Blackwell Ltd.

Hamilton, E. (1940). *Mythology: Timeless Tales of Gods and Heroes.* New York: Mentor.

Lagasse, P. (2017). *The Columbia Encyclopedia.* New York: Columbia University Press.
Accessed at credoreference.com via University of Western Australia Library license.

Leeming, D. (1994). *A Dictionary of Creation Myths.* Oxford: Oxford University Press.

Lönnrot, E., (Compiler). (1963). *The Kalevala: or Poems of the Kaleva
District.* Cambridge, Mass: Harvard University Press.

Lynch, P.A. and J. Roberts (2010). *African Mythology A-Z,* (2nd edition).
New York: Infobase Publishing.

March, J. (2008) *The Penguin Book of Classical Mythology.* London: Penguin Books.

McLeish, Kenneth. (1996). *Bloomsbury Dictionary of Myth.* London: Bloomsbury.

Mhiti, J.S. (1969). *African Religions and Philosophy.* London, Heinemann.

Reed, A.W. (1978). *Aboriginal Myths: Tales of the Dreamtime.* Sydney: Reed Books Pty Ltd.

Seal, G. & White, K.K. (2016). *Folk Heroes and Heroines around the World*, 2nd Edition.
Santa Barbara: Greenwood.

Smith, W.R. (1970). *Myths and Legends of the Australian Aboriginals.*
Sydney: George G. Harrap & Company Ltd.

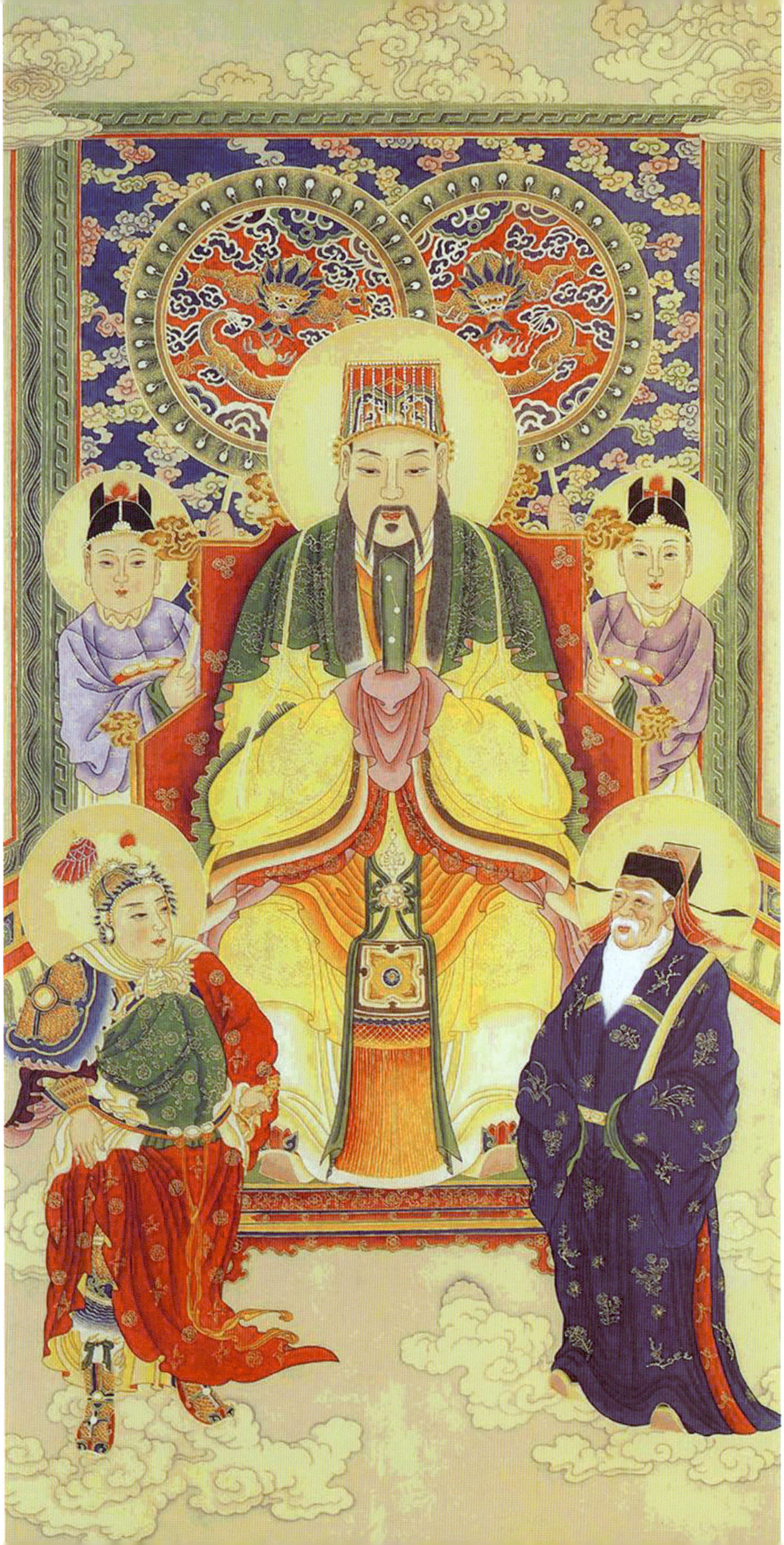

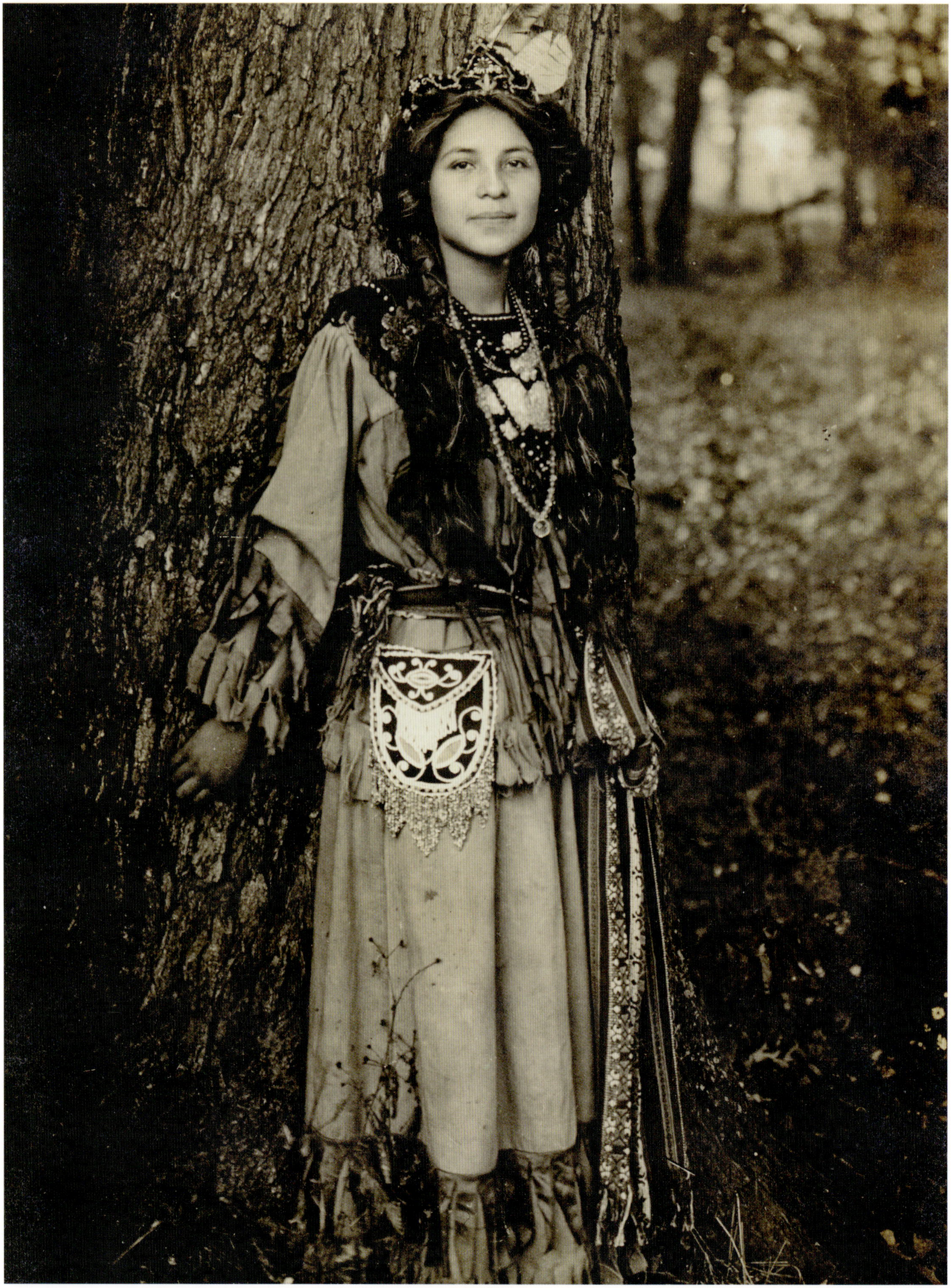

Picture Credits

AKG Images: 70, 72, 106, 167 (Pictures from History), 228 (Heritage-Images/CM Dixon)

Alamy: 34 (Niday Picture Library), 45 (World History Archive), 147 (Chronicle), 165 (Chronicle), 169 (Heritage Image Partnership Ltd.), 178 (Eye Ubiquitous), 181 (Jeff Morgan 02)

Bridgeman Images: 14-15 (The Fitzwilliam Museum, University of Cambridge), 16 (Attingham Park, The Berwick Collection, The National Trust © NTPL/John Hammond), 18 (Private Collection/© Look and Learn), 21 (Jason Edwards/National Geographic Creative), 23 (Museum of Fine Arts, Boston, Massachusetts, USA/William Sturgis Bigelow Collection), 24 (©Tarker), 25 (Louvre, Paris, France), 26 (Private Collection/The Stapleton Collection), 31 (Art Museum of Estonia, Tallinn, Estonia), 33 (Private Collection/© Look and Learn), 50 (De Agostini Picture Library/Biblioteca Ambrosiana), 53 (De Agostini Picture Library), 58 (Bibliotheque des Arts Decoratifs, Paris, France/Archives Charmet), 62 (Pictures from History), 67 (Musee du Petit Palais, Avignon, France), 71 (Private Collection/© Look and Learn), 80 (Musee Archeologique, Sousse, Tunisia), 86-87 (The Fitzwilliam Museum, University of Cambridge), 98 (Private Collection/The Stapleton Collection), 101 (Leeds Museums and Galleries/Leeds Art Gallery), 113 (De Agostini Picture Library/G. Nimatallah), 120 (The Stapleton Collection), 123 (Private Collection/Peter Newark American Pictures), 126 and 139 (Museo Horne, Florence, Italy), 144 (© Christopher Wood Gallery, London, UK), 156 (Museum of Fine Arts, Houston, Texas, USA/Gift of Alfred C. Glassell, Jr.), 170 (Louvre, Paris, France), 172 (Private Collection/© Look and Learn), 173 (British Library, London, UK/© British Library Board. All Rights Reserved), 176 (Louvre, Paris, France), 180 (Private Collection), 184 and 188 (Bibliotheque Nationale, Paris, France/Archives Charmet), 187 (Musee des Beaux-Arts, Strasbourg, France), 189 (Historiska Museet, Stockholm, Sweden), 199 (De Agostini Picture Library/M. Seemuller), 202 (Bibliotheque des Arts Decoratifs, Paris, France/Archives Charmet), 213 (Private Collection), 217 (Pictures from History), 222 (Pictures from History), 226 (Private Collection/© Look and Learn/Illustrated Papers Collection), 232 (Private Collection/Archives Charmet), 233 (Bibliotheque des Arts Decoratifs, Paris, France/Archives Charmet), 245 (Musee du Petit Palais, Avignon, France), 251 (Pictures from History), 256 (Musee des Beaux-Arts, Strasbourg, France)

Getty Images: 2 (Dea/G. Dagli Orti/De Agostini), 9 (Mondadori Portfolio/Hulton Fine Art Collection), 12 (Dea/G. Dagli Orti/De Agostini), 36 (Universal History Archive), 74 (Buyenlarge/Archive Photos), 75 (Lynn Wegener / Design Pics/First Light), 77 (Penny Tweedie/Corbis Historical), 85 (Mondadori Portfolio/Hulton Fine Art Collection), 90 (Werner Forman/Universal Images Group), 95 (Print Collector/Hulton Fine Art Collection), 96 (Angelo Hornak/Corbis Historical), 118 (Bettmann), 119 (Wade Davis), 122 (Culture Club/Hulton Archive), 125 (Universal Images Group), 132 (Universal History Archive/Universal Images Group), 138 (Stefano Bianchetti/Corbis Historical), 140 (Heritage Images/Hulton Archive),

150 (Joel Saget/AFP), 152 and 163 (duncan1890/ DigitalVision Vectors), 183 (Dea/G. Dagli Orti/De Agostini), 179 (NurPhoto), 203 (Dea/G. Dagli Orti/De Agostini), 207 (Stefano Bianchetti/Corbis Historical), 227 (Gallo Images), 230 (Nomadic Imagery/Moment), 240 (Eric Lafforgue/Art in All of Us/Corbis News), 241 (Godong/robertharding), 242 (duncan1890/ DigitalVision Vectors)

The Metropolitan Museum of Art: 10 (Gift of Thomas H. Guinzburg, The Viking Press, 1979), Florence), 18, 87 (Purchase, Alain and Marie-Christine van den Broek d'Obrenan Gift, 2009), 88 (Gift of Samuel P. Avery, 1897), 89 (Rogers Fund, 1906), 94 (Gift of Cornelius Vanderbilt, 1880), 103 (Gift of J. Pierpont Morgan), 104 (Harris Brisbane Dick Fund, 1947), 108 (Fletcher Fund, 1919), 110 (Rogers Fund, 1968), 111 (John Stewart Kennedy Fund, 1915), 112 (Purchase, Gifts of Irwin Untermyer, Ogden Mills and George Blumenthal, Bequest of Julia H. Manges and Frederick C. Hewitt Fund, by exchange; and Rogers and Pfeiffer Funds, 1982), 137 (gift of Thomas H. Guinzburg, The Viking Press, 1979), 142 (gift of Junius Spencer Morgan, 1919), 143 (Fletcher Fund, 1987), 145 (The Elisha Whittelsey Collection), 149 (gift of Dr. J. C. Burnett, 1957), 159 (John Stewart Kennedy Fund, 1910), 175 (The Elisha Whittelsey Collection), 186 (Bequest of Harry G. Sperling, 1971), 190 (Gift of Henry Walters, 1917), 193 (Mary Griggs Burke Collection, Gift of the Mary and Jackson Burke Foundation, 2015), 201 (Rogers Fund, 1920), 214 (Rogers Fund, Transferred from the Library, 1941)

National Gallery of Victoria: 20 (© Courtesy of Warnayaka Art Centre, Lajamanu)

Shutterstock: 17, 27, 28, 29, 30, 32, 35, 40, 41, 46, 48, 49, 51, 52, 54, 59, 60, 61, 63, 64, 66, 68, 69, 73, 74, 76, 77, 79, 81, 82, 83, 84, 91, 92, 97, 99, 100, 102, 105, 109, 111, 116, 121, 128, 129, 131, 133, 135, 135, 141, 151, 154, 155, 155, 157, 161, 162, 168, 174, 183, 191, 192, 194, 195, 198, 200, 204, 206, 209, 211, 212, 215, 216, 219, 219, 220, 221, 223, 223, 224, 229, 231, 234, 235, 236, 237, 238, 243, 243, 245

Wikimedia Commons: 22, 37 (Yves Picq), 38 (Museo Nacional de Antropología), 39, 42, 43 (National Palace Museum), 44, 44, 55 (National Palace Museum, Taipei), 56 and 65 (Wägner, W. [1886]. *Asgard and the gods.* London: Swan Sonnenschein, Le Bas & Lowrey.), 93 (The Blessing Studio, Salamanca, New York, United States), 107 (Guerber, H. A. [1909]. *Myths of the Norsemen from the Eddas and Sagas.* London: Harrap.), 114 (Uffizi Gallery), 115 (Hungarian National Museum), 115, 115 (Museo Calouste Gulbenkian), 117 (Musée Granet), 117, 124, 130 (Jean-Pol Grandmont), 134, 136, 145, 146 (Mabie, H. W. [1908]. *Norse Stories Retold from the Eddas.* New York: Dodd, Mead and Company.), 148 (posted to Flickr by WL), 158 (British Library), 160 (JJ Harrison), 161 (NASA, ESA, AURA/Caltech, Palomar Observatory), 164 (Illustration by Stephen Reid from Rolleston T.W. [1910] *The High Deeds of Finn and other Bardic Romances of Ancient Ireland.* London: George G. Harrap and Co.), 166 (Gift of Mrs. Russell Sage, 1910), 177 (Osama Shukir Muhammed Amin FRCP[Glasg]), 182, 196 (State deposit 07/07/1925), 197 (Ateneum, Helsinki, Finland), 208 (illustrations by F. Kellerhoven from Lacroix, P. [1873] *Les arts au moyen age et a l'époque de la renaissance.* Paris: Library de Firmin Didot Frères), 210, 218 (The British Library), 239 (illustration by Ivan Bilibin), 248 (The Blessing Studio, Salamanca, New York, United States)

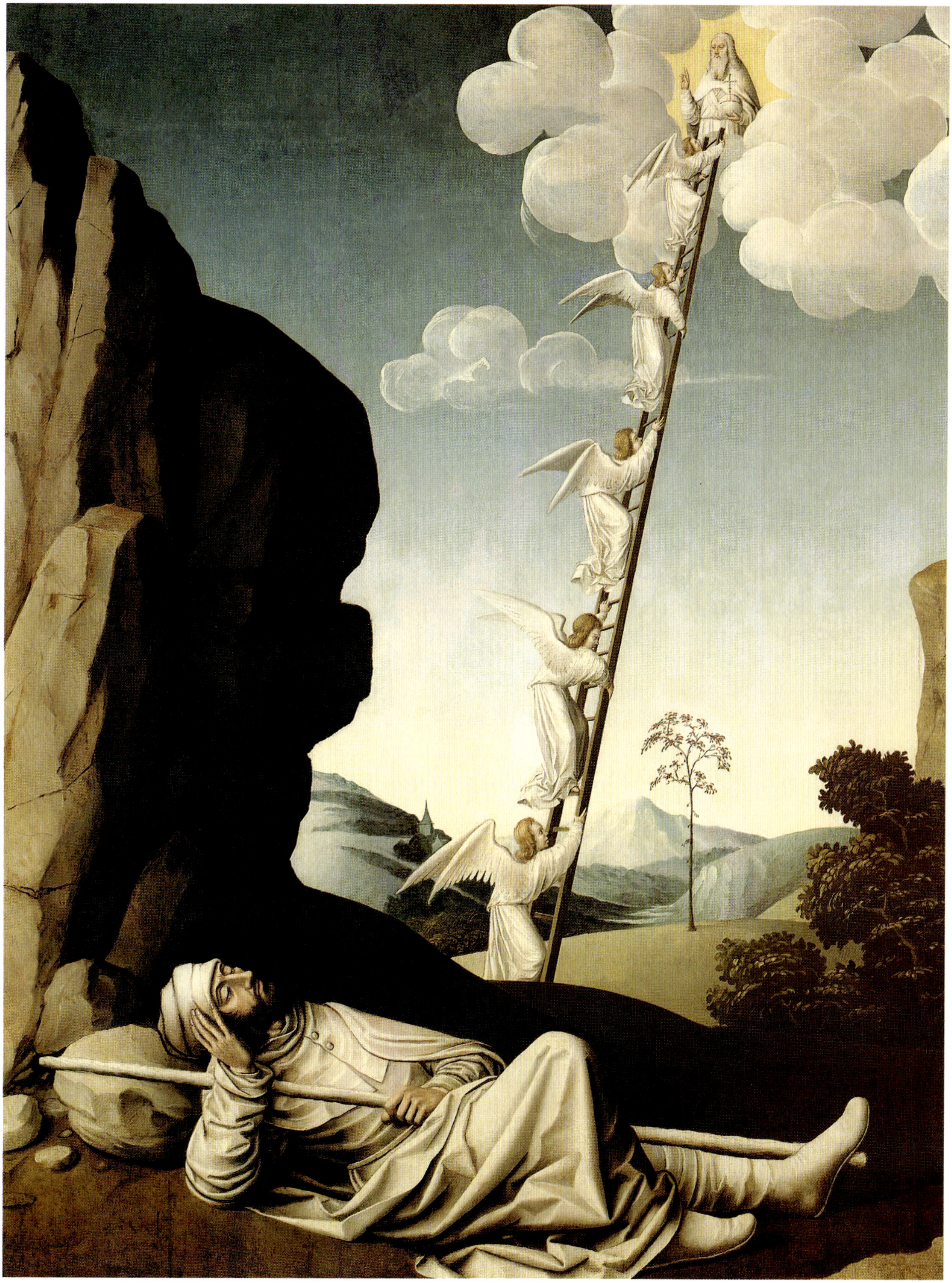

Index

Achilles 82–3, 87, 174
Adam and Eve 40, 60–1
Aegeus 128, 216, 217
Africa see also Congo, Dogon, Ghana and Yoruba
    afterlife myths 198-9, 202-3
    Voodoo 240–1
afterlife myths
    Africa 198–9
    Ancient Greece 190–1, 200–1
    China 194–5
    Finland 196–7
    Japan 192–3
    Norse 188–9
    world mythologies 186–7, 202–3
Agamemnon 86
    play 41
Agni 34, 35
Ahura Mazda 58, 59
Amaterasu 193
Amazon 119
Ame-no-minaka-nushi 22
Amenotokotachi 22
Ameta 37
Amulius, King 214, 215
Anansi 156–7
ancestor worship 242–3
Animism 230–1
Anningan 69
Anshar 26
Anu 26, 177
Amphitrite 81
Aphrodite 86, 89
apocalypse myths 144–9
Apollo 89, 190
Ariadne 88–9, 128
Artemis 89
Arthur, King 208–9
Asclepius 41, 112
Asena the Wolf 218–19
Asgard 106–7, 189
Asuras 96–7
Athena 86, 130, 216
Athens 216–17

Atum 25
Australia
    afterlife myths 202
    creation myths 20–1
    serpents in 40–1, 41
    sky ladder myths 66
    time in myths 77
    trickster myths 160–1
Ayca 206
Aztecs
    creation myths 38–9
    serpents in 41
    sun myths 68
Balder 147
Balor 98, 99
Beowulf 172–3
Brahma 110–11, 148
Bran the Blessed 212-13
Branwen 212, 213
Britain 162–3, 180–1, 208–9
Caribbean 240–1
Cassandra 41
Cerberus 201
Ceridwen 121
Charon 201
China
    afterlife myths 194–5
    ancestor worship 242, 243
    creation myths 36
    creature myths 132–3
    customs 228–9
    dragon myths 142, 143
    fortune telling 232, 233
    great flood myths 54–5
    history in myth 222–3
    moon myths 69
    sky ladder myths 66
Christianity
    apocalypse myths 144, 145
    cosmological myths 60–1
    dragon myths 142
    gods myths 108–9, 114–15
    spirit myths 139
Cipactli 38

Clytemnestra 41
Coatlicue 38–9
Congo 72–3
cosmological myths
    Christian 60–1
    Congo 72–3
    North American 74–5
    Scandinavia 64–5, 70–1
    Zoroastrian 58–9
    Yoruba 62–3
Coyolxauhqui 39
creation myths
    Australia 20–1
    Egypt 24–5
    Aztec 38–9, 41
    China 36
    Estonia 30–1
    Finland 28–9
    India 34–5
    Indonesia 37
    Japan 22–3
    Korea 42–3
    Mesopotamia 26–7
    Polynesia 32–3
creature myths
    China 132–3
    North American 150–1
Cronus 80, 84, 94
customs
    China 228–9
    North America 226–7
Cuzco 220–1
Day of the Dead 243
Demeter 100
demon myths 139
Devas 96–7
Dionysus 88–9
divination 232
Dogon 124–5
Dracula 138
dragon myths 142–3
Dreamtime myths 20–1
Ea 26
Egypt

afterlife myths 203
creation myths 24–5
gods myths 102–3
sun and moon myths 68, 69
Electryon 129
England 162–3
Enkidu 177
epics
   Greece 86–7
   Ireland 178–9
   Mesoamerica 182–3
   Mesopotamia 176–7
   Scandinavia 172–3
   Wales 180–1
Eros 89
Estonia 30–1
Ethniu 99
Europe 158–9
Eurydice 190–1
Feng Shui 228–9, 243
Fenian Cycle 210–11
Fenrir 147, 189
Finland
   afterlife myths 196–7
   creation myths 28–9
fire myths 44–5
folk stories
   common features 16
   definition of 14
Formorians 98–9
fortune telling 233
Freya 70, 189
Garden of Eden 40, 60–1
Geb 25
Ghana 156–7
Gilgamesh 41, 176–7
   Epic of Gilgamesh, the 41, 176
gods myths
   Egypt 102–3
   Greece 80–8, 94–5, 100–1, 104–5, 112–13, 114–15
   Christian 108–9
   Hawaii 90–1
   India 96–7, 110–11

Ireland 98–9
Judeo-Christian 114–15
North American 92–3, 117
Norse 106–7
Grandmother Spider 150–1
great flood myths
   Chin 54–5
   Korea 50–1
   North American 52–3
   Noah and the Ark 48–9
Greece
   afterlife myths 190–1, 200–1, 203
   dragon myths 142
   epics 86–7
   fire myths 45
   gods myths 80–8, 94–5, 100–1, 104–5, 112–13
   history in myth 216–17
   heroic myths 128–31
   serpents in 41
   sun and moon myths 68, 69
Grendel 172–3
Gun 55
Gwion 121
Hades 84, 95, 100, 190, 200–1
Haemosu 43
Hainuwele 37
Hallowe'en 179
Haumea 90
Hawaii 90–1 *see also* Polynesia
Heavenly Civil Service 194–5
Hector 83
Heno 92–3
Heo Hwang Ok 42
Hera 99
Hercules 129, 130–1
Hermes 41, 84, 130, 201
Hero Twins 183
heroic myths
   Greece 128–31
   Japan 134–5
   Poland 141
   Russia 136–7, 140
Hine Nui Te Po 33

history in myth
   Britain 208–9
   Greece 216–17
   Rome 214–15
   China 222–3
   Inca 206–7, 220–1
   Ireland 210–11
   Turkey 218–19
   Wales 212–13
Hoenir 71
Homer 83, 86–7, 128
Horus 102–3
Hrothgar 172–3
Huacas 234–5
Huizilopochtli 38, 39, 68
I Ching 233
Igor, Prince 140
Iliad, The 83, 86–7, 128, 174–5
Ilmater 28–9
Inca 206–7, 220–1
India
   afterlife myths 202
   apocalypse myths 148–9
   creation myths 34–5
   gods myths 96–7, 110–11
   time in myths 76
Indonesia
   Animism 230
   creation myths 37
Inuit
   afterlife myths 203
   sun and moon myths 69
Io 116
Ireland
   epics 178–9
   gods myths 98–9
   history in myth 210–11
   trickster myths 164–5
Isis 102–3
Island of Creation 24–5
Italy 214–15
Ivan, Prince 136
Ivan the Fool 168–9
Izanagi 22, 23, 192–3

Izanami 22, 23, 192–3
Jade Emperor 194–5, 222–3
Jacob's ladder 66, 67
Jalandhara 97
Japan
    afterlife myths 192–3
    ancestor worship 242
    creation myths 22–3
    heroic myths 134–5
    moon myths 69
    trickster myths 166–7
Journey to the West 132–3
Judeo-Christianity 114–15
Kagutsuchi 192
Kalevala 28–9, 196
Kalevipoeg 31
Kamimusubi 22
Kane 90
Karen people 230
Kingu 26
Kishnar 26
Kitsune 166–7
Kluskap 44
Korea
    creation myths 42–3
    great flood myths 50–1
Koschei the Deathless 136–7
Kotoamatsukami 22
Krak 141
Lahamu 26
Lahmu 26
legends
    common features 16
    definition of 14
Lehua 91
Lelawala 92–3
Lemminkäinen 28
Leprechauns 164–5
light myths
Loki 107
Loomislaul 31
Louhi 29
Mabinogion 180–1, 212
Mahuika 33
Malina 69
Manco Capac 206–7, 220
Marduk 26–7

Marya the warrior 136
Maui 32–3
Maya
    apocalypse myths 145
    time in myths 77
Mbiti, John 62, 63
Medusa 41, 129
Merlin 209
Mesoamerica
    see also Aztecs and Incas
    epics 182–3
    Huacas in 234–5
Mesopotamia
creation myths 26–7
dragon myths 142
epics 176–7
Mexico 243
Mimir 71
Minos, King 216–17
Mokele 72–3
Mokulaka, Chief 73
Monkey King 132–3
moon myths 68–9
Mordred 209
Mormons 236–7
Mount Olympus 104–5
Mulua Satene 37
myths
    authenticity of 15
    common features 16
    definition of 14
    function of 17
Namu Doryeong 50–1
Nanabozho 52
Nena 39
Ngapa Jukurrpa 20, 21
Njord 71
Noah 48–9
Norse
    afterlife myths 188–9, 203
    apocalypse myths 145, 146–7
    cosmological myths 64–5
    gods myths 106–7
    tribal gods 70–1
North America
    ancestor worship 242

    cosmological myths 74–5
    creature myths 150–1
    customs 226–7
    fire myths 44
    gods myths 92–3, 117
    great flood myths 52–3
    seasons myths 74–5
    shamanism in 122–3
    sun myths 68–9
    trickster myths 154–5
Nostradamus 145
Nukumi 44
Nun 25
Nut 25
Nyame 157
Odin 71, 107, 147, 189
Odysseus 82, 87, 175
Odyssey, The 86–7, 128, 174–5
Ohi'a 91
Okuninushi 134–5
Okuninushi No Mikota 134–5
Olodumare 62
Olympians 94–5, 104–5
Ometechuhtli 38
Orpheus 190–1
Osiris 102–3
Pan 112
Pan-Gu 36
Papatuanuku 116–17
Parvati 97
Pele 90–1
Peleus, King 82
Pendragon, Uther 209
Persephone 100, 101
Perseus 129
Poland 141
Polynesia *see also* Hawaii
    creation myths 32–3
    sky father myths 116–17
Popol Vuh 182–3
Poseidon 80–1, 94, 95, 128, 216
Prajapati 35, 96
Prometheus 45
Psyche 89, 201
Ptah 24
Qi of Xia 55
Quetzalcoatl 38, 39, 41, 236–7

254   *Index*

Ragnarök 145, 146–7
Ranginui 116–17
Re 69
reincarnation myths 202–3
Reynard the Fox 158–9
Rhea 80, 84
Rhodes 81
Rig Veda 34
Robin Hood 162–3
Rome 214–15
Romulus and Remus 214–15, 232
Russia *see also* Siberia
    heroic myths 136–7, 140
    trickster myths 168–9
Samyuk Yusa 42
Scandinavia 64–5, 70–1, 106–7, 146–7, 173–4, 188–9
seasons myths 74–5
Selene 69
serpent myths 40–1
Set 102–3
Seven Macaw 182–3
shamanism 118–23
Shiva 97, 110–11, 148–9
Shu 25
Siberia 118 *see also* Russia
sky father myths 116–17
sky ladders myths 66–7
spirit myths 139
Styx, River 200–1
Sun Dance 227
sun myths 68–9, 72–3
Sun Wukong 132–3
Suro 42
Susanoo 135, 193v
Suseri-Hime 135
Takamimusubi 22
Taliesin 121
Tane-Mahuta 117
Tatius 215
Tawhiri Matea 116–17
Tefnut 24, 25
Teta 39
Tezcatlipoca 38
Thailand 230
Theseus 81, 88, 128
Thetis 82

Thor 107, 147
Tiamat 26, 27
Tibernus 214
time in myths 76–7
Titans 94–5
Tithonus 89
trickster myths
    Australia 160–1
    Britain 162–3
    Europe 158–9
    Ghana 156–7
    Ireland 164–5
    Japan 166–7
    North American 154–5
    Russia 168–9
Trojan War, The 86–7
Troy 86–7
Tsuki-Yomi 69, 193
Tuatha de Danann 178–9
Tuonela 196–7
Tuonetar 196
Tuoni 196
Turkey 218–19
Typhoeus 84
Ulster Cycle 210–11
Umashiashikabihikoji 22
Väinämöinen 29, 196
Valhalla 188–9
vampire myths 138
Venus 201
Viracocha 220–1
Vishnu 97, 100–11, 148
vision quests 226–7
Voodoo 240–1
Vrinda 97
Wales
    epics 180–1
    history in myth 212–13
    shamanism in 120
Wang, Queen Mother 222
witchcraft 238–9
world mythologies
    afterlife 186–7
    ancestor worship 242–3
    Animism 230–1
    divination and fortune telling 232–3
    dragons 142–3

    fire and light 44–5
    reincarnation 202–3
    serpents 40–1
    sky fathers 116–17
    sky ladders 66–7
    sun and moon 68–9
    vampires, demons and spirits 138–9
    witchcraft 238–9
Xipe Totec 38
Yagakami, Princess 134
Yasumichi, Major 167
Yggdrasil 64–5
Yoruba 62–3
Ysengrin 158
Yu the Great 55
Yuhwa 43
Zeus 41, 45, 80, 83, 84, 85, 89, 94–5, 99, 104, 105, 112, 129
Zoroaster 58
Zoroastrianism 58–9

REDEMPTIO